Boys and Their Toys

Boys and Their Toys

*Understanding Men by Understanding
Their Relationship with Gadgets*

BILL ADLER, JR.

AMACOM

AMERICAN MANAGEMENT ASSOCIATION

New York • Atlanta • Brussels • Chicago • Mexico City • San Francisco
Shanghai • Tokyo • Toronto • Washington, D.C.

Special discounts on bulk quantities of AMACOM books are available to corporations, professional associations, and other organizations. For details, contact Special Sales Department, AMACOM, a division of American Management Association, 1601 Broadway, New York, NY 10019.
Tel: 212-903-8316. Fax: 212-903-8083.
E-mail: specialsls@amanet.org
Website: www. amacombooks.org/go/specialsales
To view all AMACOM titles go to: www.amacombooks.org

This publication is designed to provide accurate and authoritative information in regard to the subject matter covered. It is sold with the understanding that the publisher is not engaged in rendering legal, accounting, or other professional service. If legal advice or other expert assistance is required, the services of a competent professional person should be sought.

Library of Congress Cataloging-in-Publication Data

Adler, Bill, 1957–
      Boys and their toys : understanding men by understanding their relationship with gadgets / Bill Adler, Jr.
         p.   cm.
      Includes index.
      ISBN-13: 978-0-8144-7344-3
      ISBN-10: 0-8144-7344-X
      1. Men—Psychology.   2. Men—Effect of technological innovations on.   3. Men—Recreation—Psychological aspects.
   4. Recreation—Equipment and supplies—Psychological aspects.
   5. Household electronics—Psychological aspects.
   6. Technology—Psychological aspects.   I. Title.

HQ1090.A35   2007
155.3'32—dc22   2006024192

Printing number

10   9   8   7   6   5   4   3   2   1

● ● ● ● ● ● ● ● ● ● ● ● ●

*To **Richard Robin, Larry Kahaner, Eliot Applestein,**
Mark Lewyn, and **Peter Hirshberg***
because they understand, even if their wives and girlfriends don't.

● ● ● ● ● ● ● ● ● ● ● ● ●

Contents

Acknowledgments

I want to thank Lafayette Radio Electronics, a store in the '40s in Manhattan where I spent a lot of my childhood. For a boy who liked toys, Lafayette Radio Electronics was the place to be. I could get stuff there, every now and then, allowance permitting. But it was also a place of dreams: From barometers to walkie-talkies, Lafayette Radio Electronics was a wonderful land. Alas, the store is no more, replaced not as much by giant consumer electronic companies as by the rapid pace of technology.

As I write these words, cell phones, MP3 music players like the iPod, and digital cameras are beginning to become one. You can buy a device that lets you talk to anyone on the planet, lets you send that person a picture or short video of what you're describing on the phone, and then lets you listen to your favorite tunes when you're done. But while such a device is an adequate cell phone, it is only a so-so digital camera, and it is also limited in the number of songs it can hold. My brother-in-law, Richard, says it will take six years until there's a single device that does it all, but it may be sooner.

Meanwhile, between now and when all we'll need is one gadget to do everything, there will be lots of new gadgets to consume. And I want to profoundly thank all the technology companies for making all of this possible. Without Sony, Hewlett-Packard, Palm, Microsoft, Apple, Oregon Scientific, Panasonic, Black & Decker, John Deere, BMW, Nokia, LG and all the other consumer electronic, car, and gadget companies, well, I'd be spending more time talking with my family. But what about?

Still, a number of bona fide human beings helped me shape this book, and I want to take a moment to thank them. Thanks to:

> Peggy, for understanding that there's no possible way that the income for this book will overcome a lifetime of spending on gadgets.

> My children, Karen and Claire, for understanding that along with the dark side of gadgets, comes a plus: They know that they can call on me to fix their computers, a skill that's worth its weight in gold on the night before a school paper's due.

> Ellen Kadin, my editor, who was simply amazing.

> Niels Buessem, who made many of my grammatical inventions actually resemble English.

> Jeanne Welsh, who's always there in a big way when I need help.

> The people of the city of Hong Kong for undoing my writer's block.

Also, a number of people chatted with me in person and online and I want to express my gratitude to them for sharing their thoughts on boys and their toys. In no particular order they are: Julia Beizer, Brian Livingston, Andy Pargh, Gabe Goldberg, Julie Flanders, Yelena Vegera, Larry Kahaner, Richard Robin, Mark Lewyn, Fred Lewyn, Doug Ritter, Anita Baise, Nick Gimbrone, Christie Morissette, Siobhan Green, and Jim Peters. If I forgot anyone, I'm sorry, and that's probably because of a software glitch.

Introduction

M en have a special relationship with their toys—pocket tools, laser pointers, communication devices, sports gear, exercise equipment, cars, remote controls, and electronic organizers. Only by understanding how and why men have such passion for their toys, can women (or significant others) comprehend, manage, enhance, and maybe even control their relationships with their husbands, boyfriends, or lovers. And by understanding this relationship, men can also better understand themselves. Men actually don't view toys as a substitute for relationships; neither do men look at women or their relationship as if it were just another gadget. Toys are, for men, a reflection of their personality. It's commonly accepted that men like gadgets because there's no risk or worry in a relationship with a Swiss Army knife.

The relationship between men, gadgets, and women is much more complex than that—and very revealing about men.

Boys and Their Toys: Understanding Men by Understanding Their Relationship with Gadgets will explain the intricacies of the triad: men, women, and gadgets. The topics included in this book are:

✓ *The Need for Freedom.* The cell phone, smart phone, wireless PDA, and subcompact notebook computer are symbols and tools of freedom. Men need to feel that they are untethered; whether they actually use their electronic organizers, the mere fact that they own one makes men feel mobile. A man can put all his important information in a tiny device, and then just go (whether he actually goes anywhere or not.) It is the feeling of instant mobility that is important.

✓ *The Need for Power.* The laser pointer provides a feeling of power. Laser pointers are among the most popular gadgets because they give men a sense of authority, influence, strength—they are like the laser light sticks in *Star Wars*. Men want to seem powerful and gadgets often enhance that sensation. SUVs, high-speed Internet connections, and power riding mowers are also manifestations of the need for power.

✓ *The Need for Independence.* The GPS (global positioning system) is the gadget for not having to rely on anyone. The joke that men will never ask for instructions is as true as it is funny. With devices like the GPS and wireless services that provide maps, hotel reservations, and airline ticketing, men don't need to rely on others.

✓ *The Macho Need for Ego Boosting.* Toys are ego boosters. The fanciest car, the smallest video camera, the most expensive (or function-laden) watch, the fastest computer—all of these let men boast without having to utter a word. In their youth, many men used to crow about their sexual conquests; these gadgets are a safe substitute (or addition) for that. Men use gadgets to impress each other. Sword fighting, arm wrestling, and drinking contests are out as ways to prove manliness; more expensive watches and faster computers are in.

In some indefinable way, gadgets are both a reflection and

a component of men's egos. Men use gadgets to show off: Gadgets are a way to display wealth, power, intellect, and impeccable taste. But men are also defensive about their toys: When a man purchases a gadget, he's proclaiming that it's a good gadget and that his decision to purchase and use that gadget was a wise one. Criticize or ridicule that gadget, and you're criticizing and ridiculing the man. Witness this message, posted in reply to a message I posted critiquing a cell phone I'd purchased and decided to return because it was clunky to operate and had paltry memory:

> i guess i got a different model of the 8125, cuz i keep all my applications on my MiniSD and all my pics/videos/mp3s . . . and i have no memory problem. and my battery lasts all day easily with heavy usage. and apparently u didnt even try, cuz with a few minor adjustments, one handed use is a breeze.

So be forewarned: A man and his gadget are inseparable in more ways than one. Tread gently.

✓ *Gadgets Lure Women.* Or so men think. Fancy cars, multifunction watches, great hiking boots, cool stereos—all these, men think, impress women. Is a man's array of gadgetry like a peacock's magnificent tail in the eyes of the peahen? Probably not, but this doesn't change men's belief that many women are attracted by a man's gadgets, or his capability to possess many gadgets.

✓ *The Need to Fidget.* Men often have short attention spans. Men *need* to be restless. Gadgets enable men to be distracted. Television remote controls are the classic fidget-gadget. To some extent computers (and the Internet), PDAs, and cellular telephones also are an outlet for men's short attention spans. But rather than being harmful to the man-woman relationship, this restlessness can actually enhance the relationship. Men can focus their short attention spans on toys, and reserve their longer attention span time for the important things—their spouses or girlfriends.

✓ *The Need to Relieve Stress.* Playing with their toys is more than a way for men to relax, it is a way for men to calm themselves. Like women, men get stressed out, but unlike women, they don't like to talk about it. Rather than talk about their doubts and dilemmas, many men would prefer to let their problems simply slip away while playing with the latest micro-complex watch.

✓ *The Need for Novelty.* With people, this need often leads to very brief relationships. But married men—and those in committed relationships—also like novelty. However, the consequences of going out and finding a new sexual partner every week are not exactly good for the current relationship. So the newest titanium golf club, or latest radar detector (often replacing one purchased just last year), provide men with their need for newness.

✓ *The Need to Hold On to Boyhood.* When women become mothers, they get the chance to re-experience parts of their childhood by playing with their babies, dressing their children, or showing them off to their friends. Men use their gadgets to relive their childhood. As children, we had great and glorious toys, and unwrapping the latest UPS arrival reminds us of the joy we experienced unwrapping our childhood holiday presents. Few men would be seen playing with Lincoln Logs, but building a remote-controlled airplane is an adult hobby that is just as much fun as any childhood pastime.

✓ *Men Want to Look Good.* While women have makeup and diets (most diet books are bought by women) to experiment with different self-images, men have exercise equipment. Men are concerned about their body image and express this need through the use of exercise devices. Men are much less open about their need to look good; however, they are often keen on exploring how exercise gadgets can improve their looks. Men also feel that doing things like pulling a tiny cellular telephone from their pocket enhances their looks.

✓ *Gadgets Also Are an Outlet for Men's Nurturing Side.* It's their need to be a protector and helper. Alarms, flashlights, strobes, knives, and pocket tools are good examples of this. Men are quick to show off this side of their personality, too: When Niels Buessem moved into his new home, his neighbor enthusiastically bounded over, chainsaw in hand, and offered to help cut something down. Not knowing what else to say—after all, he had just moved in and wanted to establish good neighbor relations—he let him cut down a bush. "The expression on his face was child-like ecstasy," he said.

✓ *Gadgets Let Men Work and Play at the Same Time.* A fast computer, an electronic organizer, a snazzy briefcase, a travel bag with numerous compartments, or a high-tech cellular phone let men combine work and leisure. Men may be reluctant to express their need to play, claiming instead that they are workaholics. (It's manly to work 12 hours a day, not so manly to work only 7.) When work becomes fun through gadgets, men feel better about their work and themselves because they can enhance their professional life and play at the same time.

✓ *Gadgets Are Necessary Accoutrements for a Man in Midlife Crisis.* But they're not a result of a midlife crisis. The cliché portrayed in movies of a man driving off into the sunset in his shiny new sports car, which, at least temporarily alleviates his uncertain feelings, is far from the truth. By the time a man is 40 or 50, he's pretty sure of himself, and gadgets are part of his life's plan.

✓ *For Some Men, Gadgets Are a Substitute for Watching Sports.* Or at least for watching sports 24/7 (and a woman may consider herself lucky she has such a man). Not all men like watching football, baseball, basketball, hockey, wrestling, or women's beach volleyball competitions. To fill that void in time, these men fiddle with gadgets. They may be into cars, boats, radios, airplanes, computers, flashlights—whatever. But whatever they do, consider yourself lucky it's not sports. Why? For one thing, watching sports requires most men's undivided attention at a time that is completely inconvenient to his wife or partner—say Monday night when the kids need help with homework. For another, watching sports often involves the consumption of significant calories in the form of alcoholic beverages and chips. But men who fiddle with gadgets instead of sports often develop an expertise that may translate into being helpful around the house: fixing a crashed computer or repairing an air conditioner in the summer are two examples that come to mind.

✓ *Sometimes Guys Just Like Gadgets, and That's All There Is to It.* "Noticing my boyfriend turning his new flashlight on and off repeatedly I was very puzzled. So I asked him what it was about flashlights that fascinated him so, and he seemed quite pensive and could only say that they're cool and practical." That's what one woman I interviewed told me. She couldn't explain the phenomenon, and neither could her boyfriend. What's wrong with just plain fun?

What does all this mean for the relationship between men and women? It means that:

✓ Gadgets do not take the place of relationships.

✓ Gadgets do not replace sex.

✓ Men need to be boys, but won't necessarily admit to it. Modern toys let men be boys again, without ever having to acknowledge the need.

✓ Men who show short attention spans by rapidly changing television channels, for example, are merely focusing their lack of attention on an object. Letting the man
be inattentive and restless toward the Internet or TV is
better than having him let his attention wander from his
wife or girlfriend.

✓ The man who buys an expensive cellular telephone,
leather travel bag, electronic organizer, or laptop computer may not be planning to travel more often, but
rather may simply be satisfying his urge to be able to
bolt on a moment's notice. In other words, a woman
should not necessarily be concerned just because her
husband or boyfriend is acquiring the means to escape.
These gadgets give men the sense of freedom and allow
them to stay at the same time: Men can escape but not
wander away for long.

✓ Buying radar detectors, flashlights, alarms, knives, or
air purifiers is a way for men to express their feelings
toward the relationship. They imply that the man is enhancing his role of protector.

✓ Some men will use gadgets to distance themselves from
emotional contact. When a man spends too much time
with his gadgets as a means of avoiding talking about
life, what should a woman do? *Boys and Their Toys*
will address this problem.

These are some of the subjects that will be touched on in
*Boys and Their Toys: Understanding Men by Understand-
ing Their Relationships With Gadgets*. This book will help
women understand how men perceive themselves and behave
in relationships.

I want to mention something at the outset. There are going

to be seemingly sexist comments in this book. I don't plan to write anything that's overtly antigender or anything like that, but I'm sure that something I say is going to upset somebody or other because I didn't say it right, or simply because I'm making a comment about men or women. I'm sorry, but there's no way to write this kind of book, a book about gender and relationships, without somebody (and I hope it's not a book reviewer) thinking I'm a close-minded lout. But until Microsoft produces a sexism-checker that's on par with their perfect grammar- and style-checker, there's nothing I can do to eliminate all politically incorrect musings.

A final word (in the Introduction, at least; tens of thousands of words follow in the rest of the book): *Boys and Their Toys* is partly descriptive, partly prescriptive. Much of what's in this book is research and observation based: I'm reporting, analyzing, and describing what I see in the world. But *Boys and Their Toys* also offers a plan: If you know how men relate to their gadgets, if you know the place of gadgets in men's lives, you can use this to better your relationship with men, and perhaps, just perhaps, change the man in your life just a little.

How to Pick (or Adapt to) Your Man Based on What Kind of Toy He Wants

First, you need to determine if the man is a gadget guy or not. (Most men are, and that's a good thing, as you'll see.)

There's one surefire way. Peter Rojos, the founder of Engadget, one of the world's most popular gadget commentary and review websites (www.engadget.com), suggested this method to me: If somebody can date a movie to within a year or less just by the cell phones used in that movie, well that's a toy guy. Cars used to be the way that people dated movies, but ever since the police stopped using new model cars—about 1975—cars have become somewhat of an unreliable way to determine when a particular movie was made. But with cell phones: If your guy says, "That movie must have been made in 2005, since everyone was using the Motorola RAZR," then you know what kind of man you're with.

Of course, it's not the specific act of his being able to date a movie by cell phone that's significant, but the fact that he can take information that 99 percent of all movie goers wouldn't see if banged on their heads with the cell phones, and remember it weeks, months, or even years later. The major plot themes, the subtle love interests, the political implications of the movie will have vanished from his brain long before he forgets what model cell phone the various actors were using.

What other signs tell you that you've got a gadget guy? Besides the obvious ones—two cell phones on his belt and a front hallway littered with boxes that say things like Circuit City and Best Buy—that is.

A computer doesn't give you a clue. Neither does owning an iPod. Everyone has those. What books he has on his bookshelf isn't revealing either: There's simply no correlation between what a man reads (or doesn't) and his level of interest in toys.

What about cars? Sure, a fancy car is one giveaway. Same thing with a boat, airplane, and other high-priced gizmos. But most guys don't own $70,000 cars or $1.5 million airplanes.

The truth is that *all* guys like toys of one kind or another. But within that truth are many shades of gray. Not all guys like toys with blue LEDs. Not all guys like the latest and greatest of whatever it is. Not all guys read tech or computer magazines or visit those websites. Not all guys like the kind of gadgets that *I* like. I recognize this, but I have yet to find a guy who doesn't have his own favorite toy.

When I first proposed writing *Boys and Their Toys*, I made a fundamental mistake when it came to gadgets. I was only thinking about—and I'm not sure what's the best way to describe this—high-tech stuff. Fancy computers, fancy watches, fancy cars, fancy cell phones, fancy PDAs: that sort of thing. Mostly gadgets with computer chips in them. The more chips the better; the shinier the metal casing the better; the more glowing lights the better. But I was too limiting when thinking about gadgets, in part because I was reflecting on my own interests rather than thinking broadly. I had completely missed an entire realm of gadgets: tools. Power tools, power mowers, garage door openers, exotic gardening tools—that category of gadget. Toys for boys who make things. For boys who don't mind sweating. As anyone who enjoys these kind of gadgets will tell you, there's a great deal of pleasure associated with using tool-toys.

There are a number of ways to categorize boys, based on what kind of toys they particularly enjoyed as children. There's no inevitability to what kids played with and what they're destined to become (for instance I played with Lincoln Logs a lot and I have no talent when it comes to building or constructing anything). But this is a good way of classifying men because deep inside men who play with toys are still boys:

✓ Boys who want to be James Bond

✓ Boys who want to be astronauts

✓ Boys who want to build things

✓ Boys who want to be cowboys

✓ Boys who want to be sorcerers

✓ Boys who want to be policemen and firemen

✓ Boys who want to be MacGyver

✓ Boys who want to be Superman

Boys Who Want to Be James Bond

Almost all boys want to become James Bond. Not every kid, but most, at least at some point or another. Boys who want to be James Bond prefer toys that are small (PDAs), exotic (watches), fast (cars), do extraordinary things (powerful personal computers), are the latest in technology (powerful personal computers), and can do stealthy things (powerful personal computers that can do stealthy things). And for some that also may include acquiring exotic weaponry.

Of course one of the driving forces behind wanting to be James Bond has to do with getting the girl—or girls. But that's not the principal motivation.

Boys who want to be James Bond have an adventurous spirit, or at least they think they do. Obviously, not all boys (and I'm using the term here to refer to males between the ages of 10 and 90) get to live out their fantasy of being James Bond. And that's a good thing, because we certainly don't want every guy walking down the street with a Taser, encrypting all his e-mails (what a pain that would be), driving fancy sports cars (which makes carpooling with children extremely uncomfortable for the kids in the back), insisting on sitting at restaurant tables so as to always be facing the entrance, carrying scuba gear in the car's trunk, and speaking with a British accent. Although boys may truly want to be James Bond one day, by the time they're 15 or 16 that idea is tempered a bit by reality (and by a growing interest in the real world, namely girls). But part of the fantasy lives on, and in the main that's good, because it causes men to pursue the acquisition of gadgets, which is good because it brings on so many other beneficial things.

But this interest in emulating the life of James Bond does have impact, even though perhaps just in a marginal way. What it depends on is how much that Bond feeling carries on in life. What do I mean? I mean that there's a consistent tendency to acquire Bond-type gadgets throughout life: PDAs, those computers, and night-vision goggles for example.

Of all the behaviors of boys listed above, wanting to be James Bond has the least impact on what they may do as adults. There's no tendency to be a lawyer, doctor, plumber, salesman, manager, geologist, or anything else for kids who want to be James Bond. (The same isn't true for other childhood desires, as you'll see in a moment.) Perhaps there's a slightly greater chance of becoming a member of the CIA, MI6, or the Canadian Security Intelligence Service, but that aside, wanting to be James Bond can lead to any number of career paths, pretty much at random.

How strongly an adult male holds to the idea of wanting to be James Bond does influence his gadget purchases and leisure activities, however. Boys who want to be James Bond may pursue Bond-type activities as part of their wish to retain all of the characteristics that make James Bond a person to emulate: Physical fitness, intelligence, thinking on his feet, adaptability, and a facility with gadgets. Not only does James Bond *have* technology—his gadgets—but he must *use* these gadgets. Without them, you'd have MacGyver, a second-rate James Bond. Men who continue feeling a kinship with James Bond will continue to acquire Bond-type gadgets. This is a connection to all of those positive attributes that they associate with James Bond.

In other words, the gadgets are glue that binds men with all of those good things they associate with being James Bond. In some ways these gadgets help enhance a man's self esteem, but they have a deeper impact than that: They bring about strong ties to men's boyhood perceptions of being like James Bond, which, in turn, helps them continue to feel like boys. Feeling like you're 25 years younger is so much better—and better *for* you—than feeling like you're 25 years older, or even your actual age. "Act your age," is a meaningless cliché. Feeling the power, potency, exuberance, and optimism of youth is much better than being like a cliché, and an old, tired cliché for that matter.

Boys and Their Toys: Understanding Men by Understanding Their Relationships With Their Gadgets doesn't limit itself to describing men. That would be boring. This is also a book that preaches a bit. It preaches to men's significant others by saying, "let men be boys." But it also encourages men to let their boyish tendencies leak into their adult lives. Life is too short to spend it mostly as a grown-up. The main advantages of being an adult over being a child is that as an adult you get to have sex, drink alcohol, and drive cars. And driving cars, with the cost of fuel and the amount of traffic on the road, isn't so great anymore. (Sure, as an adult you get to be independent . . . if you consider independence as being tethered to your e-mail, limited to two weeks of vacation a year, and working for the IRS for a good chunk of the year.) Kids, on the other hand, get to be silly, play for half their waking day, eat lots of ice cream *without any guilt*, and acquire toys with abandon. The main disadvantage of being a child comes later, when you first encounter homework—and what a surprise that is. But homework's not bad enough to detract from an otherwise wonderful childhood.

The secret to youth isn't herbal medicine. It isn't exercise. It isn't even "thinking young." The key to a longer, happier, healthier, more fulfilled life is simply to see and enjoy the world through your children's eyes.

Decades ago, in a Rod Serling story, *Kick the Can*, several residents of a seniors' boarding house decide one day to play a children's game called "kick the can," something they enjoyed when they were kids. They start running around (sort of, since one person is in a wheelchair), kicking a can, yelling, hooting, and otherwise acting childish. There's one holdout, however: a curmudgeonly old man who stubbornly refuses to engage in these childish antics.

The others go on playing "kick the can" without inhibition. They have fun, while the curmudgeon stays in his room, trying not to listen to the running around. Then the noises change from wispy, out-of-breath shouts to high-pitched squeals—his friends have changed: They've been transformed into children, with their whole childhood to enjoy again.

Do you remember the first time you saw a rainbow? Or rode on a carousel horse? Or when you were tucked in tight while your mommy or daddy read you a book? Or climbed up the playground slide? There's nothing in an adult's life that can compare with how wonderful these experiences are to children. As parents we all get to participate in these activities with our children. But wouldn't it be wonderful if we could get to do them all over again, as if were children ourselves? To experience the pleasure of seeing a giraffe for the first time, sharing toys with your best friend, running around completely carefree, eating ice cream guilt-free, calling "mommy" and being protected, comforted, and loved?

There's a lot we can teach our children, but there may be just as much that our children can teach us. Youth has innocence, adventure, playfulness, creativity, wonder, and love.

It's one thing to go help your children down a playground slide, or even to go down the slide with your child on your lap—but it's completely different (and vastly more fun) to feel the same exhilaration, the same "whee!" that your children feel as they coast to the bottom. It is one thing to answer (or try to) "Mommy, why is the sky blue?" But it is very different to be mesmerized by this discovery.

This is all good. The various chemical and biological changes brought about by playing not only contribute to a longer and healthier life, but they contribute to a happier life, too. As the saying goes, nobody ever regretted spending too little time at the office.

You'll find boys who have emulated James Bond pursing a variety of leisure activities—some expected and some a bit surprising. Scuba diving is one of them, as is flying airplanes. So is paintball, because paintball lets you experience some of the sensations that James Bond gets to experience, without running the risk of being shot or sliced in half with a laser beam. Wanting to be James Bond has no impact on, and is not a consequence of, any particular political leaning. So the paintball thing that stems from having wanted to be James Bond as a boy can happen among conservatives and liberals alike. Such is the impact of movies, imagination, and, of course, James Bond.

Boys Who Want to Be Astronauts

Boys who want to be astronauts aren't too different from boys who want to be James Bond. They both like adventure, and they both like danger (in the abstract and at a distance, at least). And both like gadgets, of course. Boys who want to become astronauts are more gadget-oriented than boys who want to be James Bond because space exploration is (or would be if they actually got to pursue that) intrinsically the most toy-centric profession. In fact, the whole notion of being an astronaut revolves around the constant and rapid escalation of gadgets. James Bond can go out for a day or an entire mission with a set of gadgets that's more or less complete; astronauts, however, must constantly seek out newer, more capable, and more technologically advanced gadgets, especially as they encounter more exotic and hostile environments. Space exploration is an adventure in gadget innovation.

None of this should come as a surprise. Men, who as boys wanted to become astronauts, are naturally going to be gadget inclined, especially if they continue to harbor nostalgic views of the career they never had.

But there are some characteristics worth noting about boys who wanted to become astronauts. As I mentioned, they have an adventurous spirit and are more inclined toward serendipitous acts than are other men. Alas, most boys who wanted to be astronauts didn't become astronauts. But many didn't lose their desire to explore the world—that's a trait that stayed with them. They like to be spontaneous, too. The problem with boys who wanted to be astronauts is that they become comfortable in doing whatever it is that they're doing, so they may need a kick in the pants to get going.

If this sounds like a contradiction—having an adventurous spirit and not wanting to go anywhere—it's not. Boys who wanted to be astronauts are "easy dates": They're very unlikely to ever be bored, finding curiosity, amusement, and wonder in just about anything. Because they're so willing to explore whatever is immediately around them or whatever it is that they're currently doing, they can let time pass on that particular activity. When engaged—be it with a Sudoku puzzle, or a new hobby, or the idea of building a new addition on the house—these men are likely to spend hours, days, weeks, months on that. Time slips by, but they're happy about that. If you want to tap into their adventurous spirit, the latent spontaneity that boys who wanted to be astronauts have, then you have to create a spark. Want to visit Nepal? *You've* got to buy the travel books. What to check out that hot Italian restaurant? Make the reservation yourself. And don't worry too much about surprising him: Boys who wanted to be astronauts generally like being surprised.

And for that matter, they like giving surprises. You're more likely to get a surprise party with somebody like this. So enjoy.

They're not cloistered, nerdy men, though they can bit a bit more introverted than boys who wanted to be James Bond when they grew up. These are men who are intellectually curious and internally honest: They prefer to live with as few lies and exaggerations in their lives as possible. They feel uncomfortable with uncomfortable situations and believe that it's everyone's moral obligation to speak the truth. And by their being honest, not only are their relationships more solid, but the world's a better place. That doesn't mean that when you acquire a guy who once wanted to be an astronaut you get somebody who never lies, never fibs, and doesn't have any secrets to hide. Nor do you necessarily find somebody who's especially bad at lying.

What you get is somebody who'd prefer not to lie and goes out of his way to live his life without any dishonesty. And that works both ways: Boys who wanted to be astronauts prefer the company of people who are for the most part honest. Professions that require deception, such as politics and business often do, are shunned by men like this.

Boys Who Want to Build Things

There's a difference here between boys who *liked* to build things and boys who *really loved* to build things. I happen to fall into the former category: The joy I experienced playing with Lincoln Logs, blocks, Legos, and my Erector set had no impact on my adult life and was not instrumental in shaping my career path or my future personality. Indeed, if you had spied some of the creations I concocted at age six, you would have come to the conclusion that I was destined to be something—anything—other than an architect, engineer, designer, builder, draftsman, or anything else that required a steady hand and talented eye.

Of all the boyhood activities, loving to build things and being really good at it is the most reliable predictor of a career path. The proud parents who proclaim that little Nicky's going to be an architect when he grows up, based on his complicated, precise, or fanciful Lego creations, are likely to be approximately right: Nicky may become an architect, or he might become something like a bridge designer. Whatever it is, a boy who demonstrates special skills years ahead of his age is almost certainly going to nurture and advance those skills. He may become an architect, an engineer, a designer, or perhaps even something a little unexpected, such as a sculptor. Whatever it is, he's not going to be an astronaut or a spy.

Interestingly, although there's no "architect" personality type—and if there were one it would be a lot different from a structural engineer's personality—there are definite personality types that emerge from boys who liked to build things. (Although many boys wanted to be astronauts or James Bond, few boys focused on becoming architects, builders, or structural engineers, in part because six- to ten-year-olds tend not to hear or read about these professions.) How can that be—that boys who built things as kids can share personality traits as adults, while there's no set "architect" personality type. The answer is that while not all architects started out as master child builders, most boys who show exceptional talent building things at a young age end up pursuing a fairly narrow career path. In other words, not all architects played with Lego blocks, but all great Lego players become architects (or something in that ballpark).

So what is the personality type of a man who liked to build things as a boy? What are you getting yourself into when you date or marry one of those? For one thing, you get an optimist. You get somebody who doesn't just view the glass as half full, but who looks at the glass and visualizes in his head an even prettier, more exotic glass.

Boys who were master builders think that nearly every problem has a solution and that there's very little reason for pessimism or dourness. You get Tigger, not Eeyore. That means you've got somebody who's cheerful in the morning, even before coffee, and that may not be a good match for somebody who's just the opposite. Like a spring-time weather system in which cold, Canadian air meets warm, moist air from the Gulf of Mexico, this combination of cheerfulness and precaffeine dourness can cause turbulent storms in the kitchen. But if you're aware of that potential for tornadic activity in your own house, you may be able to preserve a relative calm in the mornings by doing this: Get your cheery builder-boy to be quiet. Put a newspaper in front of him. Turn the radio on to his favorite station. Get satellite radio in the kitchen if you have to. Because it's not a pretty picture in the morning in a typical family of four, when three of those four people are grumpy and one has that "let's go to the Thanksgiving Day parade" expression.

If this sounds trivial or even silly, consider this: Those twenty or thirty minutes in the morning when the whole family is together sets the tone for the rest of the day. While, in theory, it should be wonderful and calming that at least one family member's in good spirits about getting up and facing the work day (part of this attitude stems from the fact that boys who liked to build things eventually pursue careers that they really like—what's better than creating brand new structures where none existed before?), it's not. Why not? Let me put it this way: If you don't have a family member who's bright and cheerful in the morning while everyone else is just normal, count your blessings—you don't really want to know. If you do live in one of those families, you do know the answer, and my guess is that you're using a highlighter while reading this chapter. It's like having a super-rich cousin who's always reminding you how rich he is. Or like working in an office where everyone's a supermodel except for you. It's just not right.

Boys who like to build things turn out to be emotionally self-assured and steady, though tending toward the happier side of the Eeyore–Tigger scale. They're dependable and not only that, quite able to fix things at home when they break.

Boys Who Want to Be Cowboys
●●●●●●●●●●●●●●●●●●●●●●●●●

A gadget's a gadget. Not all toys involve electronics, wires, lights, and batteries, and not all boys are keenly interested in playing with things that go blink in the night. There are a substantial number of boys who want a simpler life, who want nothing to do with making things for the sole purpose of disintegrating their younger sister when she illegally enters their room. These boys want to be cowboys. They have visions of themselves in the rustic vistas of the Old West, riding horses, capturing bad guys, winning the hearts of beautiful women (whatever that means to an eight-year-old), and taming the outdoors. This translates into strutting around the house in a cowboy uniform with six guns on the side. But it also creates boys who spend a lot of time playing games outdoors, either in their cowboy uniforms or not. It's easy for a kid to imagine that the bicycle he's riding is a tall horse, that there are bad guys lurking behind trees, or that the seven-year-old girl next door is in need of being rescued. Boys who want to be cowboys climb rocks (mountains), walk over open fire hydrants (forge mighty rivers), try to capture pigeons and squirrels with their bare hands (hunt bison), and stay out till dinner time (till the sun sets over the mountains).

The cumulative effect of these activities helps make boys who want to be cowboys not only content with being outside, but uncomfortable being indoors for prolonged periods of time. They develop a connection with the outdoors that is hard to describe, but which is real nonetheless. Oddly, boys who wanted to become cowboys don't necessarily take on jobs that involve working outdoors, in part because there aren't that many outdoor jobs that connect them to the environment. Careers like geology or forestry do, for example. But if they're not able to actually work as a geologist, park ranger, or oceanographer, for instance, boys who wanted to be cowboys tend to pursue career paths that somehow involve the environment. They may work for the Department of Interior, for a company that manufactures skiing equipment, or as environmental lawyers. These kinds of jobs give them a psychic connection to the environment, even if they're unable to spend their daylight time outside.

Because men who as boys wanted to be cowboys when they grew up like to spend a lot of time outdoors, plan on vacation trips to the great outdoors, rather than to Broadway. But presumably you figured that out while you were dating, and it's one of the things that attracted you to him—his love of the outdoors.

But in the mind of a man who as a boy wanted to be a cowboy, there's not much of a difference between the indoors and outdoors. Inside is simply a better tent. That notion can have some significant consequences for family life. These cowboy men often shun certain kinds of technologies, most notably those technologies that may make your life less miserable, such as air conditioning and heat. Men who wanted to be cowboys when they were little boys see no need to master the environment in artificial ways, and as a result you find that they keep their thermostats set to 80 degrees in the summer and 50 degrees in the winter. Seriously. Some don't even have air conditioning in cities like Washington, D.C. or Atlanta, which clearly need cooling in July and August. (As a result, they tend not to get too many guests in the middle of the summer or winter.)

And why does the rest of the family put up with this? Why would any rational person—a spouse, girlfriend, or children—also want to live in a house where inside it feels like south Florida does outside in the summer? They don't want to, but boys who wanted to be cowboys have other traits that make it difficult to surmount this: They're stubborn and dogmatic. Like the pyramids of Egypt, they are unmovable. Boys who wanted to be cowboys aren't this way about everything, just about those areas of life that they perceive as being part of their core.

But on the plus side, boys who wanted to be cowboys—because they enjoy spending a lot of time outdoors and because they consider themselves to be "organic"—tend to produce nice gardens; they're often fine, creative cooks, and they are very family-oriented. Just as they feel a connection with nature, or perhaps because of this, they like to connect with their families. They especially like to spend time with their kids.

You won't find the latest and greatest computer in the home of a boy who wanted to be a cowboy. Chances are they won't have a BlackBerry either (unless absolutely forced to by their office). No PDAs, laser pointers, fancy cars, or anything like that. But one man's souped-up stereo system is another's advanced composting box or solar-powered water heater. The integration of environmentalism and technology is real, and this kind of guy not only has those gadgets, but they bring him the same kind of solace that somebody else gets from a T1 connection. These are toys that boys don't necessarily get to play with on a regular basis—you can't bring your solar water heater into the bedroom, and don't even think of trying to do that with the composter. Some men need to hold gadgets in their hands or be surrounded by them, as with a fancy sports car. But for other men, especially this category of guy, just knowing that the gadgets are doing their jobs is sufficient.

Boys Who Want to Be Sorcerers

Boys love magic and magic tricks. They think it's the coolest thing, and the first place they go when they walk into a toy store is the magic-trick rack. Magic cards, disappearing coins, finger slicers that don't, magic wands, seemingly inseparable rings, ropes that do all sorts of tricks, magic hats—these are the various acquisitions that a boy who wants to be a sorcerer or magician will have in spades. Unless he chooses to make the spades disappear. Which he could.

So what kind of gadgets does the boy who wants to be a sorcerer acquire? Actually, this particular boyhood interest can lead just about anywhere. There's no particular gadget path that boys who practice magic will follow later in life, but what's certain is that they will continue to maintain a keen interest in toys in general, because for these grown-up men, toys are a direct pipeline to their childhood. The reason for this is that it's the nature of gadgets that they transform one thing into something different: Gadgets are modern-day alchemy, and the fancier the gadget the more it appears like magic.

Take cell phones for instance: When the first phones appeared that also took short movies, that was a bit of magic. The ability to shoot a quick little movie and sent it instantly to the other side of the planet for a friend or family member to view seemed so amazing, and to many people it still is. When laser pointers arrived, they also were so amazing that people, especially men, purchased them in droves, despite the fact that their actual usefulness was quite limited: They didn't bring down enemy aircraft, but could only be used to highlight whiteboard and blackboard presentations. Flat screen televisions fall into this category, too. Just about any advanced gadget will work for a boy who wanted to be a sorcerer.

Keep in mind, by the way, that these men in all likelihood don't do any magic or own any magic tricks, but if you want to know whether somebody wanted to be a sorcerer when he was a boy, ask him if he knows any card tricks. People rarely learn card tricks later in life, so if a man knows any, chances are it's something remembered from his childhood

But what about the man who evolved from this boy? What's he's like?

Men who as boys wanted to be sorcerers and magicians are often quite different from other guys. They are fun-loving, carefree, perpetually optimistic, sometimes goofy, adaptable, and nonconfrontational. Perhaps more than any other category of guy, boys who wanted to be sorcerers and magicians like to have fun for the sake of it.

The transition from liking to do magic to wanting to be surrounded by magic naturally leads toward a lifetime ambition of wanting to goof around, to be a little less serious about something that others take too seriously. Like Hawkeye Pierce on *M*A*S*H* or Chandler Bing on *Friends*, these are people who don't necessarily turn everything into a joke . . . well, actually they do. And why not, from their perspective. Life's taken too seriously, and with few exceptions life should be pursued as an adventure, like a trek through an exotic (dare I say magical?) land with surprises, riches, and even tumultuous stumbling blocks and setbacks. The setbacks can be serious—they can range from divorce, to layoffs, to bad illness. But despite all of these problems, it helps to look at the work with a levity and perspective.

Boys who want to be sorcerers do get depressed, anxious, down in the dumps, angry, and confused just like the rest of humanity. (And when they do, you bet that they can reach into the darkest corners of their minds.) But they're not joking about stuff that might make others shuffle off to their therapist or lawyer because they feel the need to be the family clown. Instead, this is actually their psychological makeup—*they like life*. And they believe that you can turn around bad days by working at it. Humor, joking, messing around, and acting goofy—those are the techniques that these men use.

And they find that there's a self-reinforcing effect: Instead of getting angry at the Department of Motor Vehicle's clerk or the airline employee, they tell a joke, which utterly and completely disarms that person, who expected just another angry outburst. And it frequently gets good results.

It goes without saying that these men are perpetually optimistic. If you're looking at the world through a smile, that's simply how you're going to be.

These men are adaptable creatures. Bad things simply roll off of them, the way water rolls off of a duck's feathers. Their jokes and smiles and one-liners are a kind of psychic shield that helps all of the anxieties and problems in life bounce off.

These men are generally nonconfrontational. That's different from being a wimp. Boys who wanted to be magicians look for alternative approaches for dealing with problems involving other people. They prefer sidestepping the issue, rather than dealing with the ogre head-on. It's much better to cast a spell or have a trained warrior deal with the monster than have to take care of it yourself. That's what being magical is about: finding a nontraditional way of doing something.

Boys Who Want to Be Policemen and Firemen
••••••••••••••••••••••••

All boys like playing policemen and firemen: After all, what could be better than arresting your little sister and throwing her into jail—the hall closet—until she gives you what you want? That's pretty cool to be able to do. It's only later on—when boys realize that they can't simply usurp power and arrest their kid sister whenever they want or that their power completely vanishes with a more powerful entity is revealed: the parents—that they figure out that being a policeman may not be the greatest career in the world.

The fireman fantasy also gets tempered in reality and tends to die out a bit earlier than does the idea of becoming a policeman. (For some reason, parents are not too pleased with a boy who plays with fire, even if he also puts the fire out.) The desire that a boy feels to be a policeman or fireman carries through his entire life. But unless he actually becomes a policeman or firefighter, wanting to be one as a child doesn't yield a particular career path. It does, however, create a tendency toward some notable behaviors. You'll find that men who wanted to be policemen as boys are often emotional and prone to ups and downs.

They also seek out "protector" gadgets. They've never lost that desire that's actually at the heart of locking up their kid sister in the closet, which is to protect her from harm. And so, as adults, these men are likely to buy sophisticated alarm systems, powerful search lights (for finding lost children in the dark), GPS systems (for not getting lost in the dark or in the day), extra food, water, and water purification systems. All that stuff.

Boys Who Want to Be MacGyver

MacGyver is an iconic character from an old television series by the same name. He was similar to James Bond but not nearly as well-known. MacGyver was a heroic figure who saved the day through cunning, intelligence, the application of science, and the use of whatever objects were around. He never had to resort to violence to escape or to thwart the bad guys. MacGyver frequently tackled "issues" like the environment and teenage runaways.

MacGyver was very popular with boys. And many wanted to be just like him when they grew up. Because the *MacGyver* show ran from 1985 to 1992, we don't yet have a generation of grown men who wanted be MacGyver, but he had attributes that many boys emulate, such as being on the side of right and being able to solve any problem no matter how vexing and no matter how limited the resources at hand. You can't get any cooler than that.

Boys who want to be MacGyver tend to gravitate toward cool-tool gadgets, Leatherman tools,* Swiss Army knives, and flashlights. Why these? They're simple, they're not high-tech, and they demonstrate a certain willingness and ability to innovate, to fix, and to problem-solve on the fly. They tend to be politically liberal. Men who use Swiss Army knives and Leatherman tools choose these gadgets in place of sledgehammers, power saws, and crowbars. They're a gentler lot than the average male.

All of the traits that these men emulated as boys when they wanted to be MacGyver, or their era's equivalent icon, continue as adults. They're smart (they really all are), independent, self-reliant, rugged, handsome (if not in actuality, then that's how they view themselves, which counts for a lot), self-assured, and willing to take risks.

Now in case you're wondering: Yes, boys can want to be James Bond *and* a policeman or MacGyver *and* an astronaut. These desires are definitely not mutually exclusive. What does that mean? As my grandmother used to say: Oy vey! It means you have a complex character on your hands, one who can, in the vernacular of science-fiction authors, pursue one of several alternate futures.

It doesn't always go well, though, when it comes to gadgets. Although much of this book is meant to explain why gadgets are good for men and good for the relationships that men are

---

*Leatherman tools are Swiss-Army-knife-like gadgets that tend to have more tools, such as pliers, and don't break your fingernails while you're getting the tools out.

in, there are extremes, and sometimes men are unable to resist those extremes. Take the case of Tony, who clearly had multiple career objectives as a boy. According to his ex-girlfriend Donna:

> Tony uses toys as a substitute for life and relationships with humans. He devotes all of his time to becoming an expert in whatever the subject of the month is. When he hiked the Appalachian Trail, he spent eighteen months building stoves and sewing hammocks. Today he's focusing on building his own backpack for paragliding. Most guys could find a backpack in a store or online. For Tony, that would solve the problem too quickly, and then he might also have to engage with humans. Therefore, he pretends that there is no possible available solution and becomes obsessed with creating a new solution.
>
> If you took away his gadgets, he would make gadgets. I never knew how many uses there were for common objects like lids from laundry detergent bottles and pieces of aluminum. On a vacation once, we got our luggage searched because he had found aluminum pans in a drugstore that he apparently couldn't get where we lived. The airport security couldn't figure out what was in the luggage.
>
> Toys are to him what food is to other people. He doesn't care about food. But he's obsessed with gadgets.
>
> I always tell people that I trusted Tony 100 percent. Tony would never stray from me or get involved with other women —or people—because he was too busy making things, fixing things, and thinking about other uses for things. I trusted Tony because he couldn't get involved with anyone else. The fact that he wouldn't was irrelevant. He couldn't because he was consumed with doing things with stuff.

Let's hope this is a rare situation. If you see your beloved heading in this direction, take evasive action. This book will show you how.

Boys Who Want to Be Superman
• •

This may be the most universal of all boyhood desires. How many five- to ten-year-olds did *not* attach a towel of blanket to themselves and faux fly around the house? How many boys did not pursue the fantasy of being Superman, having superpowers, and especially flying? The answer is none: Every boy wanted to be Superman. Because this desire is so universal, there's really no great insight that can be derived from it. But I didn't want to exclude "boys who wanted to be Superman" from the list of boyhood desires, because that would be a glaring omission. But I will say this: Wanting to be Superman is part of the mindset that men have for their entire lives: They like to play.

Toys Lure in Women, Just Like Good Worms Lure in Fish

There are many facets to James Bond that make him somebody whom men admire and emulate, including his stylish dress, his ability to suffer all sorts of calamity and accidents without messing up his clothes, his unlimited financial resources, his British accent (if you're an American male you admire that), his cars, his great gadgets, and his clever one-liners. Of all the things that make James Bond great in the eyes of the American male, it's probably his ability to acquire alluring women that elicits the most envy. (More on the gadget side of James Bond a little later in this book.)

And sometimes this may be true. There may be some women who can be seduced or at least weakened through the exposure to a proliferation of advanced auto-dashboard consoles, sleek stereo systems, ultrashiny cellular telephones, and PDAs that can do anything and everything. But how to use gadgets to lure in women is a topic for another book. The relevant point is that men *think* that they can lure in women through gadgets, by being more like James Bond.

Deep down, men understand that they can never actually

become James Bond, but they also know deep down that James Bond is just a made-up person. (Most men know this—really! If the guy you're dating, living with, or married to actually thinks that he could become James Bond, then it's time to quietly pack a bag, grab one of his infrared high-tech LED flashlights, and sneak out in the middle of the night while his subconscious is engaged with one of those adventure dreams.)

Advertisers know this. And they flaunt it. Witness the advertisement below for an LG phone on a billboard located across from Hong Kong's "Times Square."

This is what men expect from owning the most advanced technology, be it a cell phone, stereo system, or car. Really. Men think that they all they have to do is show off their fancy cell phone and look what they get. This may be a leftover genetic trait from when humans were more closely related to peacocks.

It's not hard to explain why men think that the gadget's going to get the girl. Unfortunately, men are mostly wrong

about all of this, my wife tells me. But here we go, anyway. First, men think that gadgets display wealth and that wealth attracts women. This possibly may, in a superficial and tangential way, be the most valid of the reasons. Certain gadgets can indicate that a man has money, and certain women are attracted to men with cash. But it's only certain gadgets: Cell phones don't cut it; neither do PDAs or really any small gadgets, with the exception of some watches—the only kind of jewelry that men can get away with flaunting. Cars (as clichéd as that may be), stereo systems, and, of course, boats and planes (except for the 1960s vintage Cessna I used to fly) *may* also elevate a woman's hormone levels.

Because there are a handful of toys that may, under the right conditions, attract women—even if only on a temporary basis—men transfer this capability to the whole universe of toys. They expect that when they flash their new Pocket PC at you or show off a neat, new laser pointer you'll hop into bed with them (there's no other way to say that—that's what men think). It doesn't matter that it's painfully obvious to any outside observer that a shiny laptop computer isn't going to yield sex. What matters is what guys think, because it's the insight that we're after here.

Fortunately, men rarely buy new technologies for the sole purpose of attracting women. So that LG cell phone he's prominently displaying actually has functional purposes, as far as he's concerned. And despite the print advertisements equating gadgetry with sex, most sales people in stores don't say or even imply that a particular product will help them get the girl. So why do men think that they can use an expensive gadget to attract women? Because they're hopeful and naïve. But you probably already knew that.

Do men want women who are superficially attracted to wealth? The easy answer is that they want to date these women, have sex with these women, but they're uncertain about what kind of long-term relationship they would want to have with the kind of woman who thinks that a man in an expensive sports car is the cat's pajamas. But the actual answer is that men just aren't sure. They just don't know. They're uncertain, ambivalent, and rarely willing to reflect on this kind of question. To some extent, being able to attract women through a display of wealth is part of men's fantasies.

Men think that by buying a stylish gadget they can portray themselves as stylish, too. They're like Charlie the Tuna in the old television commercials for StarKist tuna. In these advertisements, Charlie, who for some reason *wants* to be caught and transformed into a sandwich, does a number of things to demonstrate that he has good taste, including dressing in fancy clothes. The narrator says, "No, Charlie. StarKist doen't want tuna with good taste. StarKist wants tuna that *tastes good*." Men are in the same boat, pardon the pun. They think that being stylish scores points with women, and that they can show off their impeccable taste through sleeker types of toys. I don't want to enumerate those toys here because these can be anything: Depending on the man, a stylish toy can be a cell phone, a titanium laptop computer, a shiny power mower, or even a carbon-fiber bicycle. Each man has his own kind of plumage to display.

Some toys, men think, will attract women because they show how intelligent men are. These toys fall into two categories: Toys that require thought and intelligence to operate, and toys that show that the man has a job that requires thought. In the former category you might find computer chess games, hand-held computerized scrabble programs, and scary-looking complicated GPS systems. Gadgets that somebody can't just pick up and start to use or play with. Also in this category might be anything that operates on Linux, weather radios, or just about any device that doesn't have an easily identifiable ON button.

As for illustrating that your job requires thought, it's harder to show that you use "intellectual" technology at work if you're not at work. Therefore, the way that men accomplish this is by leaving their home computer's screen on a particularly smart-looking website—perhaps complex stock graphs or chemical formulas.

Gadgets can be used to display raw power, and that also attracts women. As with many of the gadgets that men use to try and attract women ("try" being the operative word here), there's a link equating money and power, too. Fancy cars, big sound systems, big, expensive watches—the toys of power and wealth are the same things because power and wealth are inextricably linked in the minds of most mortal men.

Toys used to show off one's physical prowess are completely different from the ones used to show financial or business power. A featherweight cell phone isn't going to impress a woman if you want to show how strong you are. (A vintage 1980 cell phone might, however.) When it comes to demonstrating physical prowess, it's outdoors all the way—except for indoor exercise equipment. Treadmills, rowers, elliptical trainers, weights, and even those strange-looking multiwired weight machines that you see advertised on the lesser-visited television channels are good. But unlike that shiny silver cell phone, exercise equipment needs to appear used. Exercise equipment is the only gadget type, including even power tools and power mowers, that needs to look and smell not new. As always, whether any of this stuff impresses women isn't the point; what's relevant is that men think it does, and men acquire and use these things to attract women. If we could flash bright plumage or beat our chests like gorillas, we'd do that instead.

So with the little exception of indoor exercise equipment—

gadgets that cost thousands of dollars—a man will primarily try to impress a woman with his physical strength through outdoor gadgets that, in his mind, display ruggedness and pure physical strength. These gadgets include a whole range of equipment, from ski equipment and rugby gear to snowmobiles, scuba gear, and fancy bicycles.

To the extent that men use this equipment and get exercise, then this view of women may be a healthy one, though it may result in men ending up spending more time with other men, who are pursuing the same activities, than they do with women. You've got to love the irony.

It's the rare man who thinks that women are attracted to men who like conversation, who like to pursue mutual interests. But some men think that this conversation should revolve around technology: What you get is a guy who's deeply into gadgets and who really, really, really loves to talk about them. Dinners, long walks in the woods, ten-hour flights to Hawaii, all spent in deep, uninterrupted conversation about GSM versus CDMA cell-phone technology, secure Windows OS networks, and booting Apple computers in either the Windows or Mac operating systems. Good thing, I suppose, that the airplane windows don't open.

Men have heard vague things about how women like conversation and how talking is good for a relationship, so they figure that by acquiring and using gadgets they'll have a nexus for conversation. The good news is that any gadget can serve as the foundation for a long, meaningful conversation. But that's also the bad news.

Toys Prevent Boredom and Thus Prevent Insanity (on the Part of Everyone That Bored Guys Come into Contact With)

Men need to fidget. Men have short attention spans.
For instance, while I'm writing this chapter, I've also been checking my e-mail every few sentences, visiting CNN's website, just in case there's some breaking news that I *must* know about, and importing a couple of new CDs into iTunes. My kids are out with my wife today, Sunday, while I'm vigorously writing nonstop (except for checking my e-mail and CNN every three minutes or so), and I'll probably end up having lunch by myself, which is okay because when my family's around, they're just not too keen on my eating, reading the paper, and watching TV at the same time. (I try to explain that I'm not really doing several different kinds of things at once: That would be eating, reading the paper, having CNN on mute with captions, and listening to National Public Radio all at the same time.)

I'm not sure about why men need to fidget, but it is not

only incontrovertibly true, but it is also one of the most striking differences between men and women: You don't have to go farther than the television remote (a.k.a. "the clicker"*) to see this difference, which I'm not even going to describe at the outset. If you don't know the different ways men and women watch television, then you've either never been in a relationship—ever—or the only people you've ever gone out with shun television. Because you have to know. If you're a guy and you've got the television remote in your hand, you're happy. If you're a guy and your girlfriend, wife, or even a casual acquaintance has the remote in her hand, you're miserable, fidgety, bored, and maybe even a little tense. (I honestly don't know how women feel when guys are in control of the clicker and I dare say that most men either don't know and don't want to know: We don't want to get into a discussion of this because we don't want to hear the women's perspective, lest we have to relinquish control of the remote because they're right or equally bored, but in a different way.)

And although I still haven't described how men use the television remote differently from the way women do, I'm sure that you're reading this as if you know the difference. (If you're thinking, "Men hold the clicker in their left hand and women hold the clicker in their right hand," let's add "never watched a sitcom" to the list of reasons why it's possible—though un-

---

*A bit of television trivia: Why is the remote called the clicker? It's for the same sort of reason that we say "dial" a telephone. Telephones used to have rotary dials, and still do in some countries. Early television remotes, circa the 1960s, used sound to change the channel. These rudimentary remotes had hard-to-press buttons that *clicked* when you pushed them down. They were called "the clicker," and the name's stuck. Oh, and one other bit of television trivia: These early clickers operated in the hearing range of the sound spectrum, which means that televisions sometimes changed channels when the dial phone rang.

likely and hard to believe—that you don't know how men use the remote differently from women.)

Let's consider a possible change to the television remote: an automatic scan feature that hops from channel to channel automatically until commanded to stop. And imagine if it were possible to "lock" the clicker with a code that would keep the television moving from channel to channel until the secret stop code was entered. Wow. That would be heaven to men and hell to women. Right? No, wrong. It's two completely different things to have the television hop from channel to channel and to surf with the remote in your hand. Women don't need to fear that television remotes will be promoted with an automatic scan feature, as long as the marketing people in television manufacturing companies remain on the ball. The reason for that is that this need to channel surf comes partly out of boredom but also partly out of a deep need to fidget. The two are related and are inextricably intertwined. Men are easily and frequently bored, but they also have a need to squirm, to fiddle.

Men also *fear* that they will become bored: They anticipate boredom with great dread and go out of their way to prevent that from happening. Being bored is like being trapped in a cage, where all you can do is pace back and forth. Men channel surf at high velocities because they like it (pure and simple, they do), because they can't think of anything else to do and there's nothing really to watch among 200+ channels, because they need to use the television remote as a pacifier, but also because they're afraid of becoming bored. Men channel surf at a speed that subliminal advertisers would admire, in part because they're afraid of this: "Hon, can you go back a channel (or 10)? There's something I want to see." And men know exactly what's going to happen: They're going to end up in a dull "woman's movie," otherwise known as a "chick flick," and there they'll remain for the next 90 minutes. Here is the order of what men want to do when it comes to watching television with their spouse or girlfriend:

1. Watch sports—any sport, an old James Bond movie, or anything with Arnold Schwarzenegger
2. Channel surf and surf and surf, passing by sports, Bond movies, and anything with Arnold in it

   .

   .

   .

99. Watch a chick flick

That rapid speeding through the television dial is an act of self-preservation. Being bored isn't good for one's mental health. Just look at experiments with rats that are placed in boring environments: Both their physical and mental health deteriorate rapidly. (How scientists can determine the kind of environment that rats find stimulating is something that's too complex for this book, but suffice it to say that scientists *know*.) Some people find that playing chess or doing crossword puzzles keeps them mentally sharp (and scientists have found that problem solving can help stave off Alzheimer's disease). Rapid channel surfing may not necessarily preserve and improve men's intellectual edge, but it does help thwart boredom, which can have very negative effects on men.

I know what you're thinking. Wouldn't solving a Sudoku or crossword puzzle be a more positive, more beneficial activity for men than hyperfast channel surfing? I'm willing to say, "perhaps." But we're talking about the environment in which men find themselves: in front of the television. Men are adapting and acting in their own self-interest in *this* environment, in this reality. Somewhere else, men might, in fact, be doing a crossword puzzle, but here, lying down in bed, rapid channel surfing is what men *must* do to prevent harm that might come about from watching *Thelma and Louise*.

I don't expect that women will forever relinquish control of the remote once they understand that channel surfing is what helps keep men in tip-top mental condition, but it's useful to understand the "why" behind channel surfing: It's more than just a need to fidget; it's a way of alleviating and preventing boredom.

Magazine publishers have taken this to heart, too. Many magazines, and not just men's magazines, have significantly increased the number of short articles at the expense of longer articles? Why? It's not because men have a short attention span, though they do; it's because the worst thing is to be stuck on a train or plane with a magazine that just has a few dull articles that you didn't know about at the time you purchased the magazine. (How could you know that the articles would be boring before you purchased the magazine?*) Having a lot of very short articles allows men to channel surf the magazine: They can flip from paragraph to paragraph, each time encountering a new story, just as they hit a new channel every time they press the channel-up button.

It's a common misconception to equate multitasking with working hard. Men and women both multitask, but often for different reasons and with different desired results. First, what is multitasking? The term *multitasking* came about during the personal computer revolution of the early 1980s. Early computer chips were bad at allowing the computer to do more than one thing at a time, but starting with the 386 computer chip,

---

*Everyone, at one time or another, has picked up a "great" or "classic" book to take with them on train, plane, or bus trip, only to find that the book was dull beyond description. And there they are: stuck with that one and only book. It's an unpleasant situation to be in, and this is something that men try to avoid during every waking hour.

part of the Intel series that began with the 8088 and then the 80286 chips, computers could do more than one thing at the same time, such as computing a spreadsheet, downloading data, and letting you use the word processor. Computer chips that could allow that were called multitasking chips. The term was soon adopted to apply to people who could perform several brain-intensive activities at once. (Though not necessarily all well: I once listened to a state legislator who thought he could drive and be on a radio program at the same time—that is until he was heard, on the air, crashing into a parked car.)

Women multitask when they need to do several things at once. The demands of work and family life are such that multi-tasking becomes a necessity every now and then. It may not be fun, it may not yield the highest quality work, and it may not be sustainable for long periods of time—but multitasking can be necessary.

Men, on the other hand, multitask because they're bored. Multitasking for men often comes in many flavors and is feasible now because of gadgets, but men multitask always for the same reasons that men hold down the channel-up button on the remote like they're pressing the trigger on a machine gun to keep the bad guys at bay. Men are compelled to.

Before the golden age of gadgets, men had to rely on less-technology-advanced devices to stave off boredom, to allow themselves to fidget. Pens were good; fancy watches that you could stare at helped. Stereo systems with gauges and dials, although not portable, were also something that men could manipulate while doing something else.

In the old days cigars where the preferred toys for men. The Freudian implications aside, it's easy to see how a cigar could be a pretechnological gadget that men could play with: The shape and size of a cigar give men a sense of potency. The cloud of smoke that cigars produce, which is thick and noxious to nonsmokers, acts as a shield, a kind of perimeter defense against anyone the cigar smoker doesn't want to deal with. The smoke gives the smoker control. Cigars are accompanied by several gadgety accessories, starting with the lighter.

At the risk of writing an entire book entitled, *The Meaning and Symbolism of Cigar Smoking, 1900 to 1905*, let me say that cigar/cigarette lighters have always been imbued not only with significant symbolism, but with sexual innuendo. Lighting somebody else's cigarette also implied sex (as opposed to romance). But when a woman ignites a man's cigar—well, even a Fellini scene with a train entering a tunnel can't compare.

Old lighters weren't at all like the disposable ones that most people are accustomed to. They could be made of precious metals or they might be monogrammed. Lighters had to be filled daily. Lighting the lighter was a two-step ritual, which was an art form in itself, especially when you had to light the lighter when it was breezy outside: First, the top gets flicked back (all lighters had tops); then a cupping of the hand, or perhaps the lightee's hands were cupped; then the quick thumb pull that engaged the flint and started the spark. The ritual and the act of using a lighter, both in movies and in the real world, was an important part of smoking a cigar.

Cigars had (and still have) other gadget accessories, too: There's the metal hole puncher, which is needed to put a little hole in the cigar's tip—these can be inexpensive, or, as you can imagine, the ones made of gold can be quite costly. And they come in a variety of flavors: hole punchers, straight cutters, and wedge punchers.*

And don't forget cigar boxes. Although simply designed, cigar boxes are attractive, yet mechanistic. Not only are there

---

Cigar Aficionado magazine is a hot magazine. In some ways it's the quintessential gadget magazine.

the boxes that the cigars themselves come with, but there are aftermarket boxes, some made of exotic woods, that were, and still are, available and collected.

Pipes, too, are gadgets from pre–computer chip days. Pipes not only have their own set of gadgety gear, but pipes themselves are gadgets. There's a nearly infinite variety of pipes available, from rustic-looking corn pipes to sophisticated pipes made with a variety of expensive materials. With a pipe you can—or rather, could—instantly present an image of yourself to strangers.

There's an interesting difference between cigars and modern day gadgets: Cigars, much more than even fancy sports cars, have both gender and sexual aspects to them. There's little more masculine than men in a wood-paneled room smoking cigars together. Conversely, there's little else that compares to a woman lighting a man's cigar in the way of sexual innuendo. And that may be because there are so many other venues for sexual innuendo today that didn't exist half a century ago: Sexual imagery, sexual symbolism are everywhere, and cigars are no longer needed either as way to engage sexual tension or as a prelude to sex.

Of course sometimes a laser pointer is just a laser pointer.

Cigars' gadgetness is now passé. And it's certainly clear that the age of the microprocessor has made life much easier, more enjoyable, and safer for men by allowing them to thwart boredom and fidget wherever they are.

Although it's possible to use virtually any boy-toy for multitasking (with some exceptions such as power saws, where the consequences of divided attention can be painful), computer and communications devices are best for a couple of reasons: First these devices can often be operated, or partially operated, with one hand. Second, and perhaps more significantly, computer and communication devices do a little thinking for you:

They spell check, they find driving directions, they download financial data, they look up addresses just by typing in a few letters of somebody's name. These gadgets are designed to operated on half or even one-quarter of a brain and don't require any mechanical dexterity for safety purposes. That's not to say that multitasking with computer and communications devices is perfectly safe, but at least making a mistake with one because of inattention doesn't result in your possibly losing a finger, as might happen with power tools. (Though if you're multitasking with your BlackBerry, Treo, or e-mail program and accidentally send a steamy love note not just to the person you're having the secret affair with but to the entire office, you might wish that you'd lost a digit instead. This has happened.)

Have you noticed how squishy a lot of computer keyboards are? Soon after I bought a computer with a multitasking chip, I purchased a keyboard manufactured by a company called Omnikey. This was a great keyboard: It had a solid—dare I say "manly"—feel to it. The Omnikey keyboard was heavy. It was designed to replicate the feel and feedback of the premier typewriter, the IBM Selectric. When you pressed the keys you not only felt like you were typing, but it sounded like you were typing: solid and complete. With the Omnikey keyboard you knew that you had pressed a letter—there was no ambiguity. So great was this keyboard that I bought a spare, because one day I knew that it would fail, just as all mechanical devices do, and I couldn't imagine writing without one.*

But I had a problem using the Omnikey keyboard, stemming from the quite substantial click it made when a key was depressed: I couldn't use my keyboard while talking on the tele-

---

*Lest you think I'm some kind of Luddite, I want to remind you that this typewriter-like keyboard is attached to a computer. It may have the solid, stalwart feel of a typewriter, but it's still a computer keyboard.

phone. I want to come clean about that: I replaced my wonderful, potent, Omnikey keyboard for one of those common, run-of-the-mill squishy keyboards that let me type silently so that I could—occasionally—talk on the phone while doing something else. This wasn't a voluntary act on my part: I was compelled to replace the keyboard because I'm a guy and am compelled to type and talk. I'm not sure if I wish I were different, and I think that most men feel the same way: Would it be better not to be compelled to fidget to avoid boredom? Perhaps. But what might be nice and what's possible are two different things.

If you happen to be somebody who knows me as a friend, relative, or colleague, then you might be thinking to yourself: Does Adler feel the need to use his computer keyboard when he's on the phone with me because *I'm* boring? No—and this applies to men in general. Multitasking, fidgeting, doing several things at the same time does not reflect at all on the person who's being multitasked at. It's all internally generated, something genetic, something that men are compelled to do regardless of who they're with, and something that's made more possible because of technology. Although it's almost certainly going to be the case that the recipient of the multitasking/fidgeting/boredom prevention behavior reacts as if that's because of them, that's almost always not the cause. It's not a reaction to you; it's us. This is a situation in which that often-used cliché/lie, "It's not you, it's me," is singularly true when it comes to what appears to be a man paying attention to multiple gadgets at the same time. Men can train themselves not to fidget with their toys—it's a Zen kind of thing. I've met both of these people.

Naturally, the question arises: What did grown-up boys do before they had toys to fidget with and to help them alleviate their boredom? How did they fidget and multitask and play when they should have been paying attention to you or be deeply committed to a telephone conversation? I wish I could say that men drew complex art or diagrams while on the phone; that they played with their slide rules while in meetings; that they took their pulse with their watch's sweep second hand while chatting near the water cooler. And that, in the days before the remote, they rotated the television dial (something you had to do at the television itself) at about 60 rotations per second. But they did none of that: Before there were toys that boys could use to deal with boredom, they didn't do anything at all (with the exception of cigars and pipes and perhaps doodling).

Perhaps men listened more. Or perhaps they watched whatever their wives or girlfriends wanted to watch on television. Maybe they had no choice but to offer their nearly undivided attention. To borrow from the marines: They had to suck it up and focus on whatever, and more importantly, on *whomever* they were talking to. Yes, it was a simpler, gentler time before microcircuits gave boys these antiboredom toys. Perhaps men were bored back then, before Bill Gates and Steven Jobs and the folks at Intel made it possible for men to seek refuge from having to focus on one thing at a time. But they—we—dealt with not being able to multitask because we had no alternative, no way to escape having to mostly work on one thing at a time and talk to one person undistracted. Boys didn't have other, nongadget ways to distract themselves back in the old days. They simply didn't. It was a simpler, and more primitive, time.

In a strange and probably unfortunate way, this means that men are evolving and adapting to the proliferation of toys, and not necessarily in a fruitful way, depending on your perspective. While it's impossible to conduct a retrospective survey of men's attitudes toward boredom in the 1940s, 1950s, and 1960s, and ask them how they may have dealt with a need to fidget way back when, it's clear that gadgets are changing men. Let me repeat that, because it's one of the most important sociological revelations of the century, and a significant philosophical underpinning to this book: *Gadgets have changed men.* They have affected the way men behave alone, at work, and in their relationships with family, friends, and lovers. It's possible that toys have simply unleashed dormant qualities in men, and it's possible that gadgets are rewiring men's brains. Either way, the phenomenon is real: In the first part of this new millennium, men are behaving differently than they did just a few decades ago, and this behavior is a direct result of toys.

These changes stand in contrast to the impact of social networking sites like MySpace, del.icio.us, YouTube, and Facebook, which are affecting mostly younger people. There are substantial societal changes that these online social networks are having, which I think comes down to two changes in the way people interact and behave: First, there's great willingness—again mostly among people under 30—to not only meet strangers online, but to seek them out. MySpace, Facebook, Livejournal, Flickr, and similar social networks are successful in part because people do have a desire to encounter and make new acquaintances and friends. In fact, the entire definition of what constitutes a friendship is changing: Many people think of people they've never met or spoken with as their friends, and indeed many of these friendships seem to have strong emotional bonds. Their friendships are genuine and as substantive as many real-world friendships.

Indeed, people tend to "talk" to each other online much more frequently and much more intimately than they do in the real world. Although I'm past 30, I have to say that I find these social networks alluring and fun. They're a good way to meet people with similar interests and to let serendipity into your life—something that's often lacking in the physical world. How often during a day or even a month does chance or a random encounter affect our lives, making them more interesting. I'd say almost never. But in cyberspace, random and directed encounters do affect our lives, and often in positive ways, if we have the will power and fortitude to ignore and walk away from the bad apples that also exist in cyberspace. (In other words, there are a lot of nuts, unpleasant and even bad people in cyberspace.)

In many ways, the success of MySpace–like websites is closely related to the boy-toy-boredom phenomena. Kids (again, mostly younger people) seek out websites like MySpace because they're fundamentally bored. Boredom shouldn't be viewed in the negative way it's often thought about: Boredom is a gap, a void, that people want to fill. Boredom leads to activity of some kind, and what that activity is can either be productive (engaging in conversations online, for instance) or unproductive (checking e-mail on your Treo every two minutes). Boredom is like a meteorological low-pressure system: If there's something available to eliminate boredom, people will make use of it, be it MySpace or spell-checking while on the telephone.

The MySpace phenomenon is also a product of a new generation's willingness to shed privacy. I want to mention that here, because it stands in contrast to the kind of gadgets that men use when they need to fidget, when they're bored or distracted. MySpace, Facebook, Livejournal, Blogger, and other social Web services in many ways encourage users to shed their privacy. In previous generations people would be horrified if anyone read their private journals or diaries; many people who use online social networks essentially put their diaries online for everyone to see. The toys that boys seek to thwart boredom are not like MySpace at all when it comes to giving up privacy; there are no popular gadgets that men use to fidget with that are used to reveal their private thoughts to the world.

I've come to the conclusion that men like the feeling that

comes with being distracted, with fidgeting. Men abhor the feeling of being bored—it really is unpleasant. But men do like
the—what's the best word?—buzz that accompanies fidgeting.
Boredom, which is unpleasant, leads to fidgeting, which is actually quite a pleasant neurological activity. Fidgeting fills the
boredom gap in a way that nothing else can. Talking on the
telephone can't do it; attending a meeting can't do it; chatting
with your spouse or children sometimes can't do it. It's got to
be fidgeting and only fidgeting that replaces boredom. And I
think that this has to do with the fact that there are certain
neurological changes that accompany fidgeting that are not unlike being high or intoxicated. (Or that out-of-focus jet-lagged
feeling that puts you at a distance from the real world.)

Fidgeting enables men to de-focus, to feel slightly detached
and out of step with what's going on around them. In that way,
fidgeting is a relaxing, stress-relieving activity, even when it
accompanies some other activity, as it usually does. Fidgeting
lets men deal with the world in a less stressful way than they
would otherwise have to by adding a pleasant feeling to the
day. Drinking might accomplish the same thing, but it's less
acceptable to drink during the workday than it is to fidget.
(Drinking at home after work is okay and often done as a fidget
substitute.)

Gadgets are a benign, cost-free (once the Visa bill is paid),
and occasionally even productive way of alleviating boredom.
Gadgets that work best at this are those that can be operated
with one hand, as I mentioned earlier. They're also gadgets that
can be operated silently and with a minimum of flashing lights.
(Why product designers like to add bright LED lights to devices
is a mystery to me. My office resembles a light show when the
overhead light is turned off, and if I had my computer, printer,
backup drives, Treo charger, and all the other peripherals in
my bedroom, as some people must have, I would need to com-

pletely cover all the LEDs with black tape in order to be able to get to sleep.) Many gadgets are able to help men accomplish this, including those that you might think would be too bothersome, such as cell phones. But now that cell phones can surf the Web silently, they've also become perfect fidgeting devices.

Men don't multitask with their gadgets because they have a large workload; men don't play with their gadgets while doing other things because they want to procrastinate. Men *need* to do this. It's part of their psyche. Or at least it is now that gadgets make fidgeting a lot easier and a lot more varied than just clicking a pen.

Picturing a man talking on the phone, sending his e-mail on his BlackBerry, and glancing at a report on his desk all at the same time yields an image of a hard-working, multitasking guy. But this is actually just the face of somebody relieving his boredom by fidgeting with his toy. It's hard to do several things at the same time, especially if you want to do them well or even correctly. Doing something with a gadget in hand may be portrayed by Hollywood as symbol of working hard, working productively, and working nonstop: enterprise fortitude, to coin a phrase. But that's not the case at all, except for the fact that men don't mind being perceived as workaholics. (There's some kind of merit badge that men think they get for arriving at work before the pigeons come out of the trees to feast on fallen muffin crumbs, and for staying at work past the hour that food delivery services stop bring people their dinners.)

Toys do help contribute to this self-perception, but that's not even a secondary purpose to what's called multitasking. Men are compelled to fiddle with their toys while they could, and probably should, be giving their undivided attention to something else. The benefit they derive from appearing to be skilled multitaskers and workaholics only reinforces their playing with certain kinds of toys while at work: Fidgeting with—

juggling—several different technologies at the same time at the office not only makes them *feel* good, but they think that it makes them *look* good, too. As the cliché goes, it's a no-brainer. There are too many positive reinforcements not to.

There's another driving force behind this desire to play with toys anywhere and everywhere: Men tend to have short attention spans:

Very short.

Like a couple of seconds.

Or less.

That's one of the reasons that magazines and newspapers are gravitating toward brief articles.

Men are more comfortable dealing with information in tiny bits.

Men prefer short summaries, "executive summaries," rather than long analyses.

It's just the way they're wired.

So what does that mean? It's another force driving men toward playing with gadgets during meetings, while on the telephone, while somebody else is driving the car, and while carrying on a conversation at home. The gadget interjects a pause into a longer activity. Rather than having one 20-minute meaningful conversation, playing with a toy during that conversation (which ironically may turn a 20-minute chat into a 30-minute conversation) breaks the activity up into perhaps five 5-minute conversations: And that's easier for men to deal with. Gadgets introduce a rest period into whatever men are doing. Men rely on gadgets to help them cope with certain aspects of life in discrete, smallish chunks, which from a guy's perspective makes life not only more manageable, but actually manageable.

You can see this behavior in a number of different areas—it doesn't just manifest itself overtly in playing with toys while doing something else. Men will often have the television on mute with closed captioning displayed. They'll look at the TV every now and then while talking with you (or while on the phone). This helps break up whatever primary activity they're engaged in. You may even see a guy have a television on mute with closed captioning and the radio on as well. He's not necessarily absorbing information from two different sources; he's breaking up the radio's news with periodic glances at the television. From his point of view, this is not only perfectly normal, but it's also perfectly necessary. Otherwise he may be forced to concentrate too long on one single thing.

There's one advantage to the fact that men have very short attention spans and need to fidget with gadgets while they're supposed to be giving you their undivided attention. (Has anyone *never* had a conversation with a male person who's also fiddling with his PDA or who has one eye on the computer monitor?) Every now and then a man is actually able to give you his undivided attention, to focus entirely on what you're saying and doing. It doesn't happen all that often and it may in fact be a by-product of the fact that he's actually bored with the Internet or with whatever toy is the gadget du jour. When that happens, when he's able to look you in the eye when you're talking, you'll temporarily forget about all those other times when he's half engaged in the conversation; now you think that he's the most caring, interested person you've ever met. It impresses because it's such a contrast to his usual behavior. Another reinforcing behavior.

Men Need to Be Spontaneous, and Toys Offer a Safe Way to Maintain Their Youthful Spontaneity

The sine qua non of adolescence is spontaneity. But it's spontaneity without any regard for the possible consequences. Acting impulsively and seemingly dangerously and insanely is something that teenage boys and young men do regularly, and that's why there are proposals every now and then to ship all boys age 15 to 25 to Greenland for the duration. The list of things that boys and young men do that are crazy is nearly infinite: They're things that, if you survive, send visible chills down your spine when you recall them decades later. From redlining the speedometer in cars to using alcohol in ways that brought about the decline of entire civilizations to "pranks" at school that nobody thinks are funny—boys will do absolutely scary things without hesitation.

Why? Because it's fun. Not just that they think it's fun: it *is* fun. Mature adults don't view it as fun, but perhaps some of us, in our more honestly reflective moments, can remember that

acting spontaneously, no matter the danger or possible repercussions (which were never on our mind), was fun. Incredible
fun. I'm sure that if you removed and analyzed the brains of 17-
year-old boys right after they used fishing line to go bungee
jumping off a 300-foot-high bridge, you'd find a giant amount
of endorphins and other feel-good chemicals in their brains.
Most adults wouldn't repeat the things that they did as teens
and in their twenties (and our lower backs might not allow us
to try those things again), but we can appreciate the strange
magnificence of taking giant risks at the spur of the moment.
Again: Back then, we didn't view those activities as risky. It was
the exhilaration that we enjoyed, and especially the spontaneity. In fact, it was in large part because these things were done
spontaneously that we were able to do them at all: If we thought
about them or (shudder the thought) asked our parents for per-
mission, we'd simply have stayed at home, fiddling with our
stamp collections. And that would have been no fun at all.

Whereas I firmly believe that everyone likes spontaneity
and doing something new and different every now and then,
I'm also sure that everyone copes with risk differently, or prefers not to take any risks at all. Not everyone bungee jumps,
flies gliders, goes rock climbing, shoplifts (not all risky things
are good things), uses marijuana, has sex in public places, trav-
els to dangerous parts of the world, and walks over hot coals
with their bare feet. Some people prefer stamp collecting or
reading in front of the fireplace to risky adventures, and that's
perfectly normal, too. To be fun, spontaneity does not have to
be combined with physical risk. Spontaneity can be enjoyed
solo, as in giving or receiving a surprise birthday party; hop-
ping on an airplane for Paris at the last minute; throwing out
your Windows computer and buying an Apple (the converse of
that *would* be too risky, however); quitting your job to become
a freelance something; trying a new, exotic restaurant instead

of an old standby; calling up an ex-boyfriend or girlfriend with whom you haven't spoken for decades; rearranging the furniture in your bedroom and surprising your spouse (well, there may be a physical risk here); or getting in your car with a week's worth of clothes and just driving and seeing where you end up.

I recently came back from a trip to Hong Kong and China that I took with my 15-year-old daughter. What was different about this trip is that we planned it less than a week before we left. Usually when I take an overseas trip, it's something I agonize over months in advance, in part because it often takes months to plan a distant journey, especially one to the other side of the world. The trip came about because my wife suggested that Karen and I go somewhere while her sister, because of other commitments, stayed home to study. When Peggy suggested this, I'm sure she was thinking that we might go to New York City, or go skiing in West Virginia. When I said, "Hong Kong"—a destination picked not quite at random, since my daughter's best friend's family had moved there—it took Peggy a while to become accustomed to the idea. But we did it: A trip just about as far away as you can go, planned just about as spontaneously as was possible.

Being spontaneous isn't easy. For one thing, it often takes time away from everything else you need—or think you need—to do. Sometimes being spontaneous takes money. It almost always takes going against what you've planned or regularly do. Being spontaneous is a somewhat rare occurrence, despite the fact that it's often great fun. Spontaneity makes you feel young again. I'm sure of that. Tell friends about something spontaneous that you've done and watch their faces—you can actually see the envy appear across their smiles. And it's more than just the feeling of being you that results from being spontaneous; being spontaneous can actually make you more youthful. You see this in yourself whenever you return from doing something that's on the spur of the moment: When you're done, you're more physically fit, have more stamina, sleep more soundly, and perhaps even are more sexually fulfilled and fulfilling.

But we generally lose that spirit of spontaneity as we get— dare I say it?—older. Certainly there are time and money constraints to being spontaneous, and when you're older, more mature, and more seasoned, you have responsibilities to your family, to your business, and to your coworkers. You simply can't up and go. Although I'll discuss the meaning of the Black-Berry later on—the BlackBerry is that little gizmo that lets you (makes you?) access your e-mail everywhere—these constraints on us have nothing to do with technology. (Technology can, in fact, be somewhat liberating if you use it judiciously.) These constraints are simply a part of life.

The problem is that the more we're hemmed in by work and family (and I'm sorry if "hemmed in" has such a negative sound to it), the more we get used to it. It's like using an alarm clock: Once you start getting used to one, you're not going to be able to get up on time without it. I'm not judging anyone, including myself: This just simply is the way life works. We get into a pattern and we get used to it. It's reliable, if not comfortable, and those conditions are also pleasant in their own ways. Reliable, comfortable, steady—sure, it's good. But it's not sufficient. Nobody just wants to collect stamps. There has to be more going on in one's life, lest your imagination and drive dwindle away. Without spontaneity men wither away, becoming just like peanut shells, with nothing inside. And nobody wants that, right?

Besides these real constraints on being spontaneous, another reason why adult men are frequently reluctant to act spontaneously is that they confuse spontaneity with impulsiveness. How to clarify the differences between spontaneity and impulsiveness? It's one of those things that you understand intuitively when you see it but may be exceedingly difficult to describe with precision. *Spontaneity* involves doing something on the spur of the moment, without any or much planning. It often involves doing something different, something that you haven't done before or don't usually do. *Impulsiveness* is the same thing, only with the added kicker that you could get yourself into a lot of trouble, arrested, or killed. Here's an analogy: Spontaneity is buying a Porsche; impulsiveness is "borrowing" your father's Porsche one evening after he's gone to sleep to see how fast you can drive it on winding mountain roads.

That's where toys come into play. Toys let guys be spontaneous without having to spend much money (really!) and with little risk. Toys let you do what you need to do, what's necessary for a fulfilling life, without all the complexity that a trip across an ocean or going for a solo trek across Death Valley would entail. While toys are not a complete substitute for real-world spontaneity, they are a good temporary measure, until you can book those tickets for the Orient Express.

Which toys? How are these toys deployed? That depends on the individual guy, but perhaps the best way to show how these toys work when it comes to giving men an outlet for spontaneity is by looking at computer games. Good computer games—and to the credit of the computer gaming industry many games fall into this category—have an element of mystery and surprise to them. I personally don't play many computer games, but I have played a few and find that they can be alluringly spontaneous, especially those games where you don't know what's lurking around the corner, or you don't even know the rules of the game. Games like Adventure (one of the first labyrinth style games, text-only, where you have to wend you way through a maze containing dangers and riches) and Myst®, a game that involves, well, you don't really know, because that's the essence of the game: New and unexpected things happen, if only you can figure them out. A lot of computer games have monsters and things coming at you that can kill you (or your character); but games like Adventure (which is free these days—just Google it) and Myst help promote a *feeling* of spontaneity because everything that can happen is going to be unexpected and probably something that you can't even imagine.

Realism isn't important or even necessary when it comes to computer games that exude spontaneity. In fact, realistic action computer games probably aren't the best games for this at all, because you know what many of the possible outcomes and scenes are: The monster jumps out from the dark, the race car crashes, the enemy helicopter gets shot down, the fair maiden gets rescued, somebody dies. Many computer games, while not predictable in every regard, are predictable in many of their components. What happens to you or your character is a result of how good you are at manipulating a sword with a mouse or a fighter jet with a joystick. Pull back on the stick too hard and your fighter stalls or the wings get pulled off—no big surprise there.

A lot of computer games involve skill and manual dexterity. Computer games can improve hand-eye coordination, which isn't a bad thing, either. But that's not the same as helping you feel the breeziness that comes with spontaneity. Here's a short list of the feeling and attributes associated with spontaneity:

- ✓ Youthfulness
- ✓ Energy
- ✓ Exuberance
- ✓ Breeziness
- ✓ Excitement

✓ Anticipation

✓ Liveliness

✓ A Sense of Wonder

It's Zen for Men. Although the term "virtual reality" connotes a sense of cheating when it comes to experiencing the real world—visiting Tibet is certainly more rewarding in every way than playing a computer game in which your character is located in Tibet—it's not the reality of the experience that's important for men. Sure, it's so much better to experience the real thing, but it's the *feeling*, the *sensation*, the *emotion* that matters here. People don't expect to have all the sensations and perceptions that accompany the real thing (if they did that would indeed be a problem) but the temporary experiences generated by artificial serendipity can be quite pleasant. That's the notion behind transcendental meditation or a glass of wine: They bring about temporary, but real, euphoria. Playing with gadgets and games that have surprise and spontaneity in them does the same thing, but there's often a social, or family, stigma attached to playing a computer game or using another gadget to relax, refresh, renew, and enjoy.

I need to take a brief break from describing more about how gadgets that include serendipity in their makeup help men. I want to talk about an aspect of this that makes it harder for men to benefit from playing with toys: *You.* Not *you* specifically, though it could be, but society in general, which casts a stigma on playing with toys. Whether "playing" is viewed negatively depends on the particular gadget. Somebody can be fiddling with his BlackBerry all day long and it's considered bold and adult. But taking a 15-minute work break in the middle of the day to play Myst would not add any points to your semiannual performance evaluation, even if it made you more productive, easier to get along with, and generally a better worker.

Regardless of the virtues of playing with toys, doing such is viewed as juvenile, nerdy, geeky, and a waste of time. And people who hold these views about playing with toys frequently don't hesitate to condemn the game and toy players whenever they feel like doing so. The upshot of this is that the beneficial elements of serendipity play take longer to manifest themselves. It's like having an argument with your spouse before you go to sleep: For every one minute of arguing, add five extra minutes to "foresleep," the amount of time it takes to fall soundly asleep.

In addition to imaginative computer games, the Internet itself can offer men an opportunity to engage in spontaneity without having to purchase a $1,500 airline ticket. Most of the Internet—or at least most of the ways that people use the Internet—doesn't help men find serendipitous moments, but it can, if used properly. Most of the time, most men (and most women for that matter) hop back and forth between their favorite two or three websites. Click, scan, click, scan. Pretty dull. And not only is it dull, but looking at the same limited few websites over and over again is a very narrow way go to through life. Dullness begets dullness: it's too easy to get stuck in a rut. And not only that, but after spending 30 minutes skipping back and forth between these few websites, we feel like we've cheated ourselves out of time: What a waste, when I could have been doing something better, something more interesting.

But what? What would that more interesting thing be? It wouldn't necessarily be visiting a website that teaches you to read Gaelic or learn calculus—that's certainly not playing, which is the essence of what this book is about and which is so important to the development and maintenance of men. The Internet has a wide range of possibilities from good to evil and everything in between. You can use it to learn something, teach somebody something, help others, stay in touch with friends and family, and, as I've mentioned, waste plenty of time.

But what about using the Internet to bring about these physical and mental changes I listed above? Men don't go to a meditation website that continually broadcasts a tonal "Om." Instead they seek out serendipitous websites such as Stumble-Upon. StumbleUpon is a social networking website, but it is quite unlike other social networking websites, such as MySpace and Facebook, which are for the most part biographical displays. StumbleUpon lets you discover new websites based on two criteria: Your own personal interests and how you rate other websites help determine what StumbleUpon—www.stum bleupon.com—finds for you next. So the serendipity is likely to be 1) a website you've never seen before and 2) something you're predisposed to like.

StumbleUpon builds its database of websites from sites that other StumbleUpon users have added—that is its social networking component. Not every website that StumbleUpon offers is dynamite and unleashes a torrent of endorphins, but because you never know what the next mouse click will bring, that anticipation and expectation is in itself fun. What Stumble-Upon does so well is that it not only enables serendipity, but makes the whole processes even more pleasurable by adding anticipation to the mix. (And I apologize if I've introduced a new way to waste time. But StumbleUpon helps you get that warm and fuzzy feeling.)

But StumbleUpon isn't the only place on the Internet that encourages serendipity. YahooGroups, Google Groups, and similar Web services are also good at this. These "groups" are places where you can meet like-minded individuals, people who are interested in what you're interested in: serendipitous encounters.

There are gadgets other than the Internet itself that lend themselves to serendipity. Though I'm not yet of an age to pursue this (and pardon the stereotype), metal detectors trolling along a beach looking for coins or treasure or anything are the quintessential example of a toy that can lead directly to serendipity and all its joys. The worth of what's actually uncovered isn't nearly as important as the act of looking and not knowing what you'll find and then finding something completely unexpected. It may look like the old men who walk up and down beaches with their metal detectors are the epitome of boredom (these thoughts come from people who are lying on the beach doing exactly *nothing* or reading a Danielle Steele novel), but they're actually actively engaged, getting a bit of good exercise, and playing with their toys in a way that makes them feel perhaps half a century younger through the pursuit of and encounters with serendipity. So next time you see somebody sweeping a metal detector back and forth while you're just soaking up rays, don't be so quick to invoke a stereotype.

Telescopes and binoculars also fall into this serendipitous category of gadgets. Even when you know what you're looking for, it's a surprise when you actually find it. When I got an advanced telescope with computer-controlled tracking I aimed it at Saturn, which I was sure had rings because I've seen pictures in books. But it's something entirely different to actually see it through your own telescope. It was amazing. The rings were so clear, so sharp. I trained my telescope next on Jupiter, using the high-tech computer controls, and was equally surprised.

Flashlights, too, are great for spontaneity—and spontaneity's close cousin, novelty. Boys like newness and often choose gadgets that are not only practical or fun, but that don't cost *that* much ("that" being a relative term) and can be replaced with newer models every now and then without causing a panicked call from the credit card company. Who's going to notice a new flashlight? To the untrained observer (the spouse or girl-friend), all flashlights look the same. Sara, one of the women I interviewed for *Boys and Their Toys* told me:

> I do not notice or feel that he pays more attention to his flashlights than me. He is very excited and energetic (like a child at Christmas) when a new flashlight has arrived in the mail. It is at this point that he'll be very focused in telling me the specs on his new flashlight and getting me to push the buttons to test it out and wait for me to give my opinion, which I find very interesting because he is much more fluent with flashlights than myself (however, over the years I have learnt a lot). I have to admit sometimes it feels like he has discovered the holy grail and all its secrets. Haha! However, I like it when he does this because I feel he is sharing something with me that is important to him. And he just seems so happy to be telling me all the specs on the flashlights that I have to admit I get excited too . . . and I am tempted to get one of my favorites from his collection for myself."

Photography, too, falls into this category. Ironically, the old, chemical-based film is more likely to give you that seren-dipity feeling than a digital camera. It's fun and surprising to find out how a picture turns out, but a big part of that fun comes with anticipation. With a digital camera you know in-stantly; with a film camera, especially if you develop the pic-tures yourself, it takes a while to see what develops. And frequently what develops is a surprise, in part because of the lag time between taking the picture and seeing the photo. It's surprising that when you have some control over the outcome, as with developing pictures or playing a computer game, that it adds even more mystery and pleasure. I'm not entirely sure why, but it may have to do with the fact that when you mix in your own work, you're waiting and wondering how you affect things. I know that when my wife pops a pie into the oven, it always turns out great, but we never know exactly how the pie will taste, and that's the serendipitous part.

Many other gadgets fall into the serendipity realm. Shortwave radios, of course, are one of those gadgets. Shortwave radios aren't as popular as they once were (popular being a relative term), but scanning the dial can yield all sorts of surprises. And, as is true of all serendipitous gadgets, it's addictive because you want to see what happens next. In fact, that's one criterion you can use to determine whether a particular gadget promotes serendipity: Is what happens next uncertain? Satellite radio, to some extent, is also a serendipitous gadget: With so many channels, tuning up and down the satellite radio spectrum often yields surprises. And AM radio, because it's so infrequently listened to, can also be a way to encounter serendipity.

I've discovered during my research that men typically prefer random (or shuffle) mode on their iPods, while women like to listen to music in the order in which they've planned it. (Can you imagine how wonderful it would be if cable television had a shuffle mode: if you could surf channels randomly!) Although I do want to avoid focusing on the differences between men and women because that would make this a different kind of book, in some instances the contrast is striking, as it is when it comes to the way men and women use their iPods and other portable music devices. This difference has a lot to do with the strong preference that men have for serendipity, for surprise: That surprises and chance encounters create all sorts of pleasurable feelings and reconnections with their youth.

A little later I'm going to write about the so-called midlife crisis that many movies portray men going through. But I want to clear up a cloud that exists around the notion of midlife crisis and why men buy expensive thing such as cars, gadgety watches, stereo systems, and boats when they're in their 40s and 50s. The short, and most truthful, answer is that it's because they can. Expensive sports cars and boats are expensive. It takes men decades to amass enough money to be able to blow it all on a car, and that happens just around age 40 or 50.

Buying expensive things isn't necessary part of a reaction to a midlife crisis; it's part of a man's natural tendency to crave spontaneity. Chip Fisher took up riding horses and polo when he was in his 40s. He just thought it would be fun. And it was, but it turned out to be more than just fun. "I could go anywhere in the world with my mallet and play polo," he said. Leaning how to ride horses and play polo gave Chip a way to be spontaneous in places where he would otherwise just be an ordinary, and possibly slightly bored tourist.

Gadgets Prevent Infidelity

I'm making this assertion as plainly and as directly as I can: Gadgets prevent men from cheating.

And this may be important news. Not because gadgets actually prevent men from straying, as if they're some kind of force field, but because they reduce the volume of little devil that lives inside each man's head that suggests the possibility.

When I first conceived the idea for this book I intended to write a descriptive, somewhat amusing, and definitely captivating book about why men like gadgets and how men's use of gadgets explains their behavior. A valuable and earth-shattering book. It was only during the course of researching and writing *Boys and Their Toys* that I came to the astounding but true conclusion that there is a direct relationship between boys and their toys and whether they cheat on their wives and girlfriends.

I'm going to take this observation one step further: Whether your man enjoys his toys is a big predictor of whether he'll eventually have an extramarital affair.

And that leads to the question: Can a woman influence whether a man is faithful by encouraging him to have toys, or more toys, or new toys, or something like that? Maybe. Read on.

Men fidget. They're constantly in motion. The old clichéd

image of a guy sitting in his BarcaLounger, beer in hand, the television on, and a quarter of one eye open, peering at a football game is just that: a cliché—and a false one at that. Guys get tired, just like women, but most of the time they need to be busy. They need a hobby. They *need* their gadgets.

When I was in high school we learned about the French Revolution, the Russian Revolution, and the American Revolution. We learned that all revolutions have the same underlying structure. In order for a revolution to occur, there must be two elements: The fuel and the spark. The fuel is the unrest and discontent that the people feel. It's their unhappiness, their uneasiness with the way things currently are. It is their desire for change. The spark is the specific event: an assassination, a new law—something that triggers a revolt. In the case of the French Revolution, the fuel was multifaceted: Dissatisfaction with the monarch was growing, food was scarce, resentment of the nobles was increasing, and taxation was burdensome and viewed as unfair. On July 11, 1789, King Louis XVI acted to consolidate power in the monarchy by banishing the reform-minded finance minister, Jacques Necker, and surrounding Versailles with soldiers. These two acts were the spark, and the French Revolution ensued.

For men there is always a spark. The potential sparks are other women. Not all women. But all women that guys talk to either in person or over the Internet. That means there are a lot of sparks out there. But so what? Men are used to seeing sparks—attractive, available women—all the time, and this includes occasional trips to the beach or swimming pool where they're wearing less clothing. Nothing, absolutely nothing at all is going to happen from these many encounters. A bikini-clad woman, sitting by the poolside and chatting with a guy, has about as much potential to cause an extramarital affair as a car filled with gasoline has of spontaneously exploding. That beautiful woman doesn't by herself contain the fuel that could ignite an affair; by her mere existence she's not going to cause an extramarital affair.

Extramarital affairs have little do with sex—at least as far as their causes are concerned. Sex may be the nexus of an extramarital affair, but it's not the precipitating cause.

What does precipitate an affair are two other things: marital tension and boredom. (If you've noticed, I'm talking just about married men here, and not boyfriends, and that's for a reason: For marital tension and boredom to creep into a relationship, that relationship usually has to have been going on for several years, which usually means marriage.) Marital tension and boredom are the fuel behind an extramarital affair. Mix an unhappy marriage with a beautiful woman, the spark—and there you've got something.

What does marital tension and boredom have to do with boys and toys? A lot.

All marriages that survive the first 48 hours (that's all marriages except those of movie and pop stars) have some amount of trouble; few marriages are perfect and pure. All marriages have their duller days, too. Ups and downs now and then are no problem for most marriages. An argument or two, a dinner at which very little is said—that kind of thing doesn't produce the same kind of fuel that inspired the French Revolution. But if there's continual marital tension (and I realize this is a vague and relative notion) *and* there's ongoing boredom in the man's life, that could be a danger. Men who are unhappy in their marriage often seek out sex outside of the marriage.

How toys figure into all of this is straightforward: Toys provide contentment, purpose, satisfaction, something to look forward to, something to play with, something to explore, to share, to enjoy. They are not the glue of a marriage, but they help the glue bond.

It doesn't matter whether you (the woman in the marriage) understand or appreciate his toys, his hobbies, his interests. Chances are that you won't understand them. Here's how the Car Guys on National Public Radio explained boys and their toys to one listener, who was calling in to complain about her husband's old, broken-down Camaro, which was just taking up valuable garage space. They said that it's his pleasure, not just because it represents a potentially new car, but because one day he will turn what looks to you like a wreck into something that works. It's junk to you, but just the opposite to him.

There's another aspect to this problem of women and men simply not understanding what makes the other tick, something I call the gadget imperative. As a woman, you may have encountered this and have thought that your man's behavior was an anomaly, but I'm here to tell you that it's not: Yes, men sometimes would rather try to fix or solve something than have sex. Let me stop for a second and say that again:

Men would rather solve a computer problem than have sex.

Of course, men don't necessarily think of it this way, and many men will be quite surprised to find their spouse or girlfriend asleep at 12:45 A.M., when they finally, finally, figured out what it is that went wrong and repaired that problem. And the men may even be a bit astonished by the fact that their significant other didn't wait up for them while they were slaving away, enduring numerous reboots, uninstalls, and reinstalls. (It's not necessarily fixing a computer that may keep a guy working all night; it could be a car repair, building a bookcase, or even getting a toilet handle properly balanced.) But whatever it is—and these days that task probably involves a computer problem—it has nothing to do with your sexual allure. I promise. (Let me issue one caveat, though: If this is the *first* time you're planning to have sex with somebody or it's your wedding night, and he's deeply engrossed in fixing the computer, then he does have a problem.)

I realize that this may be difficult to accept, but the worst thing you can do is to become angry or upset or depressed because you're being ignored or (you think) worse—that he's reacting to your sex appeal. What should you do? You can watch *Seinfeld* reruns or just go to sleep. In fact, I'd suggest heading in that direction anyway—we all could use some extra sleep, so you might as well accept the inevitable and get a head start. You can't alter his destiny, which is to fix that computer.

If the fact that your man would rather spend time with power tools than with you has absolutely nothing to say about your relationship, your attractiveness, or your sexuality, then what does it have to do with? What could cause guys—and we're talking about men here who, when it comes to sex, are frequently, well, you know—to forsake sexual relations in favor of messing around with their toys. The answer to that question is both simple and complex. It's a microcosm of everything that has to do with men. The answer is simple, because men are really primitive creatures, easy to train, and easy to predict (sort of like pet dogs); it's complex because this particular phenomenon seems to conflict with the very essence of men. At least it seems to contradict what you *thought* you knew about men.

Men need to succeed. Men do not like loose ends. Men do not like unresolved problems (as long as those problems involve inanimate objects and not relationships). Men believe that the solution to whatever the problem they're engaged in is just around the corner. And that may explain the familiar refrain: "Just five more minutes." Those are probably the most genuine, sincere words that men utter, because they do believe that the solution is at hand, especially if it's just one more computer reboot. It's also that men lose all track of time when immersed in one of these problem-solving endeavors. The same time distortion does not occur during regular hobby activities, but when men are on a problem-solving mission, for all practical purposes time moves much more slowly.

You might be thinking to yourself: Isn't it like the rat and cocaine experiment: The rat can press one of two levers. Lever 1 gets the rat cheese. Lever 2 gets the rat cocaine. The rat would rather press lever 2 and in fact continues to press lever 2 so much that it forgets entirely to eat and simply starves to death. But then where's the pleasure that men feel when working on trying to fix one of these awful problems? It's obvious that men don't derive pleasure while working on these problems, at least not in the same way that rats do from cocaine. That's obvious because of all of the *very bad words* that you can hear from the man every now and then. These are words that don't go hand-in-hand with having a good time. So this is definitely not a rat-and-cocaine kind of phenomenon.

Nor is it a masochistic fetish. Speaking from my own experience, I can absolutely guarantee that no man on earth wants to try and discern exactly how two different Microsoft programmers intended their programs to get along. No man wants to waste hours and hours just to get a computer working properly. No man likes interpreting error messages like this:

STOP:
0x0000001E—KMODE_EXCEPTION_NOT_HANDLED
and
_VWIN32_FaultPopup
and
visual c + + run time library.
Run time error:
winword.exe r6025 pure virtual function call

Don't you feel sorry for him now?

Worse, you can't even surf the net while you're trouble-shooting, because you're interrupted every fifteen minutes by an automated request to reboot. Multitasking is not possible when you're troubleshooting a computer problem. Men have to focus on the problem. The radio's off, there no television in the background—all other gizmos are asleep.

Men are not happy campers when it comes to the process of fixing the computer. No man wants to spend forty minutes on hold, only to have to focus on understanding the words behind the foreign accent after the telephone hold ends. Dealing with tech support is often just like what Rob Pegoraro of the *Washington Post* experienced:

> Seeing a chance to test how HP might handle a tech-support query—I decided to call for help. (Note: The tech-support number wasn't listed in HP's "getting started" or "PC troubleshooting and maintenance guide" manuals.) After saying a couple of words to a speech-recognition system ("monitor," "yes," "home"), I was routed to a polite rep who asked a few questions, left me waiting on a silent phone for a minute or two, and then said she'd transfer me to the right department. The phone rang, and then a moment later the call dropped. I love the PC industry! You just can't make this stuff up.

That's what guys go through.

No man enjoys looking through boxes for that right screw or trying to track down the key CD to install whatever it is that needs to be installed. None of these things gives a guy any pleasure at all. Some psychologists say that there's a little masochist in everyone, but I have yet to meet anyone who enjoys navigating a tech support's telephone system.

And yet, they'd rather do that stuff than have sex with you.

Why? As I said, it's complex. First, as I alluded to, for men time moves more quickly when they're focused on a maddening computer problem. And although the amount of time it takes for a computer to reboot is a long enough time to have sex, most men realize that their girlfriends and spouses may object to this. Besides, their concept of time is actually totally—and here's the technical term—*messed up* when they're involved with their gadgets. It's not about you: It's about *them*. It's ego, of course: man versus the machine. But it's also frustration—an emotion and feeling that is so unpleasant that it must be dealt with and eradicated as promptly and as thoroughly as possible. Men aren't always good at compartmentalizing problems: If there's something unsolved, something nagging, something that's not working right, that's going to be a cerebral sore that's only going to get worse over a short period of time.

Not all problems are like this for men: Men can procrastinate quite proficiently, when they want to. The clichéd example is men talking about their relationships, which is portrayed as something they like to avoid doing. But that's not really true. Given a chance, men often enjoy talking about "us," the future, and their feelings. But if there's something to fix, especially if that's a computer, anything else will feel like a thorn, until he fixes the technology.

Men Hate Ambiguity

You've probably seen the advertisements. Atomic watches; clocks that set themselves automatically and are accurate to a millionth of a second (really, they are!); laser-sighted levels; BMWs with doors engineered to within a fraction of a millimeter; RAZR cell phones with quad-band technology, perfect lines, and curves. These are gadgets and toys designed for and marketed to men: Men like precision. Men like things to be *exact*: If it's 12:05 P.M., then it's 12:05 P.M. and not 12:05 P.M. and forty seconds. (Don't confuse this desire for precision and exactness with the willingness or ability to be on time. Knowing and doing are two different things.)

It would be easy enough to state this and leave it at that because it's pretty clear that men enjoy exactness in life. (Truth be told, this is why many men are torn when it comes to discussing Einstein's theory of relativity at parties and elsewhere: On the one hand, there's the mathematical exactness that's an important component of this theory; on the other hand, it is called the theory of *relativity*, and that word bothers men. But I digress.)

Why do men like toys that have an abundance of precision? There are two important reasons for this. First, men deal with a lot of gray in life: There are many ambiguities and uncertainties in their daily existence, and gadgets with exactness are a good antidote to that. Second, the land of gray is often all about emotions, feelings, and talking about emotions and feelings; exactness helps to obscure that gray area in life.

The day starts out well for me, as it does for most men. The alarm rings precisely at 6:30 A.M. or 7 A.M., depending on the day's agenda. There are a few specific tasks to perform, and the next half hour mostly involves a known sequence of events with very predictable outcomes. The bathroom, the newspaper, the coffee, breakfast—there's little chance for any unexpected surprise.

But all is not well with the world. Maybe that special somebody who shares the same bed asks, "How did you sleep?" Or worse, "How did you sleep? *I* didn't sleep well." *That* statement all but begs for a response like, "I'm sorry. Why didn't you sleep well?" And that question can lead down a path that's as uncertain as a dark, wooded road in a Stephen King novel. Without warning, the world that began with certainty deteriorates into a world of uncertain grayness, growing grayer and grayer all day long—just like that Stephen King novel.

As the minutes tick by, the variables increase and life becomes what it really is: Uncertain and unpredictable. And getting worse quickly. Unfinished home work. A favorite shirt not laundered. English muffins turned shades of blue and green. The airline calling to tell you that the flight you're scheduled to be on has been canceled. The toaster (now toasting something other than an English muffin) and the coffee maker in conflict and blowing a circuit. A minibrawl over who gets the comics first.

And *who* hid your keys?

But amidst all this chaos you glance down at your Casio watch, which synchronizes itself multiple times a day with the atomic clock in Colorado, and an inner calm instantly counteracts all that ambiguity and confusion. A glance at your watch, or just the feel of it on your wrist helps restore your tranquility. The touch of your ultrafine pressurized ballpoint or the finely nibbed fountain pen in your pocket helps do the same thing in a way that's impossible to explain. Or the SwissCard in your pants pocket: The finely crafted design of this small pocket tool helps destroy the cloudiness that surrounds the world. It's as if the precision of the SwissCard, or the atomic Casio watch, or the fountain pen could cut through our Universe of Ambiguity and Uncertainty and open up a Universe of Predictability and Calm, just as the Subtle Knife opens a door to other universes in Philip Pullman's trilogy, *The Golden Compass.*

Precision toys have an even more important function for men: They help men cope with the fact that other people in their lives have emotions and are able to express them. Emotions, feelings, complex human interactions, talking about relationships—these are the gray areas of the world that men know they can't avoid. Every now and then they have to address an emotional problem, which in its own way causes emotional stress among many men. Because they can't avoid dealing with emotions and feelings, they need a refuge, a counterweight. And that comes from precision-oriented toys.

Why won't regular toys work for this purpose? Why can't a man just fire up his computer and surf the Web or take a ride on his power mower to compensate for the emotional entanglement that is family? You might think that it should work—after all, a toy is a toy. You might think it should *if you're not a guy,* that is. Not all toys are equal in the way that they affect men. Each type of gadget has a particular effect on guys, and guys seek out different toys for different reasons. It's not too far a stretch to say that certain toys evoke certain fantasies, certain projected lives, certain visions of oneself that don't really exist, but we wish they would. In that sports car you can be James Bond; with that Swiss Army knife you're MacGyver (or some completely self-sufficient, independent, able-to-do anything outdoors guy); with that new high-tech stereo system you're the cat's PJs when it comes to being cool and nouvelle; with the tiny cell phone that takes still photos and moving pictures you can be a spy (hopefully only in your mind—otherwise you could end up in real trouble).

But none of these toys balance out the rough-and-tumble emotional life that men experience during each and every ordinary day when they have to deal with somebody who actually is open with his or her emotions. Men know that at any given time they can be confronted by a family member whose eyes are welling up with moisture or who is even crying. Men try not to think about that, but they know that it can happen without warning, and, even worse, because of something they said, or didn't say. They need a quick emotional exit. A refuge. Although men don't articulate it this way, gadgets that have precise working parts or that are exactness-oriented are the emotional equivalent of a fire exit in a theater.

How is this possible? How can a toy that works so exactly be an emotional refuge for a guy? What about opening up over a few shots of whiskey at a local bar? Shooting some hoops with the guys? Taking the car out and driving real fast on a deserted country road? Don't those things help him emotionally? How in the world does a watch calibrated by a time signal from Colorado fix his psychological needs? The answer to that isn't something that is easily accomplished by a rational explanation. Anything I can say won't make sense to you, especially if you are looking for logic.

Let me try and explain this link between certain kinds of inanimate objects and a man's emotional well-being this way: Consider the vision quest, where somebody goes off on a trek alone through the woods or into the desert for days or weeks. Or someone climbing a tall, dangerous mountain. To many people, these activities make no sense: What's the fun in hanging by a thread off of a mountain peak when you can get the same great views in an IMAX movie? Yet to the person doing these things, the activity is enriching in a way that words can't describe. People don't become different people by climbing tall mountains, they climb tall mountains because it is who they are. In other words, *you're* not going to understand why they do it, but *they* understand why. It makes sense to them.

The same thing goes for men who derive comfort in devices that have a strong element of precision: It feels right to them. To you, it's either invisible, or possibly even "stupid." But just as you might not understand why anyone would want to fly an airplane upside down at 200 miles per hour, you shouldn't seek a rational explanation for this, either. The beauty of civilization is that despite our similarities, we're also quite different in many ways.

Protector Toys

How Guys Expose Their Nurturing Side Through Technology, Even if They Don't Know It

I'm not going to talk about guns. Not because I'm squeamish or pro-gun or anti-gun or anything like that. It's because men who own guns obviously have a particular motive for purchasing those guns, and that purpose may or may not have to do with protecting the family.

How you should deal with a gun in the house, or whether a gun at home is a good idea—these are questions that I'm not planning to deal with here. These are personal, political, and societal issues, and gun ownership doesn't say a whole lot about the subtle, less obvious, more interesting, more revealing, and, dare I say it, less potentially dangerous, aspects of a man's personality, the *other* stuff he has to protect his family.

Besides, not all hazards, both real and imagined, can be thwarted through firepower. There are bad guys, that's for sure, but there's also the threat of fire, choking, falls, carbon monoxide poisoning, and other accidents; there's also the danger of unexpected and unimagined medical emergencies. A neighbor's house caught fire a few weeks ago because the strong afternoon sunlight was reflected in a mirror and set some bedding ablaze. I'm not kidding. Depending on where you live there could be severe thunderstorms, hurricanes, floods, tornadoes, earthquakes, killer bees, alligators, grizzly bears, cesspools that can open up and swallow people, and more. And then there are the common, but less often fatal dangers (or inconveniences), such as power outages in summer, power outages in winter (each requires its own separate solution), leaking roofs, clogged plumbing, darkness, insect infestations, or a single bee terrorizing a house (you wouldn't laugh if it happened to you). Not all dangers happen at home either: There's everything from medical emergencies while driving, to stranger danger, to shark attacks, to malaria, to sunburns, to "the runs."

Yes, the world is full of potential catastrophe. Fortunately, there are toys and technology to the rescue. Some of these gadgets have a real and substantial prevention potential; others just enhance health, safety, and security around the margins.

I know that some of what I've written about health, safety, dangers, hazards, and emergencies may have a tongue-in-cheek ring to it—but that's just the way I write, so pay no attention to any grammatical implications. What I mean is that regardless of how real or improbable a particular danger may seem to you, what's important is how men perceive, react to, and deal with the scary, dangerous world.

Before I discuss some of the specific toys and tools that men may purchase, let me touch on something that may come up: When does a guy's interest in toys for safety and security move from being a benign hobby (in your view) to an obsession? It's one thing to get some flashlights, emergency flood lights, and glow sticks, but is it another to spend $3,000 on a backup generator? Is it the case of somewhere along the continuum of flashlights to power generator your beloved going from possibly practical to obsessed? To be blunt: Is there a line that's crossed that indicates that he's got a mental problem and needs professional help?

Although I'm not trained in psychology, I've lived a good many years and experienced a lot of different things and people, and I can tell you that everyone, without exception, has personality quirks, odd behaviors, strange beliefs, personal demons, and secrets. My feeling about whether a particular protective behavior crosses the line isn't determined by what your husband or significant other does, but what he doesn't do. Buying a $3,000 generator so that you can have lights during a once-a-year 15-minute blackout may be excessive, but it's not a big problem—unless it's taking away money for groceries or the rent. Refusing to go out to dinner because thunderstorms are predicted, or not wanting to take a trip because of the strong possibility of an ice storm, or not letting anyone in the family get a cell phone because you read a quack article about how cell phones cause brain cancer—those are problems. If your spouse's pursuit of gadgets to protect and serve doesn't significantly change any of his other behaviors or your relationship, you're okay, and so you should continue to read this book to learn more about what the acquisition and love for these gadgets means. If the gadgets and the notions behind them make him unable or reluctant to do certain normal things, then it's time to put this book down and discuss your concerns.

Now back to the fun stuff.

Men are not necessarily the emotional guardians of the family; they are the physical guardians. But this physical protection should not be taken as unemotional, unfeeling, cold, or anything like that. Just the opposite: The pursuit, acquisition, and maintenance of these toys demonstrate a man's love for his family, just like giving her a dozen roses shows his love for his spouse. A rose by any other name might just be a small array of lead-acid universal power supplies.

Men—and you probably don't need me to figure this out—aren't always willing or able to share all their feelings, and especially their worries. So they express themselves through their toys. It is their deep hope that somehow you will intuit this. In fact, it is my belief that a guy purchases certain toys—in particular those that have the singular purpose of offering safety and security—not just to actually protect his family, but to have these toys speak for him. Men often purchase protective toys as a way of communicating.

Not all human communication is verbal. We all know that. From facial expressions to impatient finger tapping, to dropping the octave of one's voice a few notches, to a light touch on somebody's arm, we all express our feelings to one another without words. So you need to know that as far as protector toys are concerned, they are a part of a man's nonverbal communication. That is a key to the way that men are: Protector toys are their way of speaking to *you*, of telling you something important about the way they feel. Men do not buy their protector toys in the abstract. And while they do buy them for their own enjoyment (more on that in a little bit), that's not the main mission of getting these protector gadgets.

There's a risk when writing about protector toys (or any gadget for that matter) of getting too involved in the intricacies of that gadget, to start writing more about the toy than the reason behind the toy, so forgive me if I get carried away here or somewhere else in the book. Besides having utility and providing psychic support, the truth is that gadgets can also be fun. So when somebody—and that's guys I'm talking about—buys a protector toy and seems also to enjoy it, he's allowed to do that.

Women often don't allow themselves to enjoy technology and don't view technology as something fun. That's partly because they sometimes resent technology—the way it steals men away from them. If it wasn't for that computer, that car, those power tools, *the remote control,* men would be discussing meaningful things with their girlfriends and spouses. (Right?) Everyone has a list of fun things to do and enjoy. Some people like opera; others hip-hop. Some people enjoy eco-tourism; others won't travel anywhere that doesn't have the words "Four Seasons" in it. Our list of things that we like is relatively short and relatively closed, and although we may try new things, we tend to prefer what we already like. Sure we may give the scallops a whirl if our favorite food is shrimp, but the jellied calf's feet—no way!

And that's the way it is with technology for women: Protector gadgets are not to be found on the list of things that most women find enjoyable. Adding technology to one's list of fun stuff, when it's not already there, requires a great deal of psychic energy, not to mention studying—ugh—as gadgetry isn't always intuitive to operate. Women also see gadgets as an expense and don't always feel that the cost of a second power mower is justified by their being able to ride side-by-side with their husbands.

Because women don't see gadgets as something that can simultaneously be used and enjoyed, they look at each thing a man buys with a critical, if not disdainful, eye. It's either thumbs up or thumbs down for that generator, motion-detector webcam, satellite phone, alarm system cellular backup, water purification system, or advanced first aid kit. And the thumb only goes up if the particular protector-gadget is 100 percent, unambiguously needed. If the specific gadget doesn't ring true as something that's going to perform an essential function then women are not likely to share or express joy with that object.

Women are often not shy about pointing out what they see as wastefulness and a certain obsessive-compulsiveness with gadgets. But pointing out that a particular protector toy is a waste of money or worse is the kind of statement or sentiment that can strike right at the heart of a guy's core. It hurts. This lack of understanding of or empathy with the reasons why a guy purchased a particular toy goes well beyond simply "not appreciating" it, as if that generator or defibrillator is just like a painting or movie that's subject to somebody's particular predilections. Everyone understands that people have a wide range of tastes, likes, and dislikes, and most people are thick-skinned enough to accept disagreement and criticism about their tastes. But when a guy buys that emergency generator he's not buying it because he likes the duct-tape-gray color it comes in; it's because he is expressing his love and concern for his family.

Men usually don't ask, "Do you like my new generator?" They don't ask the equivalent of a woman's question, "Do these shoes go with my outfit?" because the motivations behind the two purchases, a generator and new shoes, are entirely different. In fact, it's acceptable from the guy's perspective not to be complimented on his wise purchase. It's all right not to say, "Wow—that's a great idea, buying a backup emergency generator. I think that's the kind of thing we'll be glad we got one day." A guy does not need to hear that—validation in the form of a compliment isn't necessary. But—and this is crucial—denigrating the guy's purchase isn't like saying, "I don't think those shoes go well with that outfit." It's not a comment on taste or subjective perspective. It's not the same as two people having a different opinion about the dessert at the restaurant. This has nothing at all to do with subjectivity or taste or preference: The very reason behind that purchase has everything to do with the man's core values and the way that he is expressing them. If you disparage a guy's purchase of a protector toy you are putting a stake through his heart.

How can this be? How can a man be so fragile as to have his whole sense of self wrapped up in a purchase made at Home

Depot? Well, it's a little more complex than that, but that's an important fact not to forget: Sever or diminish the link between a man and his protective gadgets and it's like severing a link between a Borg and the collective.* Although you may see a guy carefully unbox the generator, make sure all the wires are tight, and be careful about getting the exact fuel need, it's not because he *needs* to keep the generator clean and polished. He just may enjoy the fact that the generator looks great (to him, anyway)—it's impressive, sturdy, has nice lines and curves and build, and its various knobs, dials, and switches add to the visual allure. But unless you happen to be very, very unlucky, he's not going to put that backup generator in your living room or bedroom. It's going to be tucked away in some dark basement corner, out of view, and for the most part the only company the generator will have is that of a washer, dryer, and hot water heater. How can somebody actually enjoy something that he's never going to use and doesn't actually look at all that much?

Adding another layer of mystery to this is the fact that he doesn't ever have to use it or turn it on (other than that initial test) to enjoy the generator—and this, in fact, may be the oddest aspect of the whole boy-generator relationship. He doesn't wear it like you do your shoes; he doesn't admire it like the painting in your front hall; he doesn't play with it like you both do with your children; he can't eat it, take it to work, or any-

---

*What the heck is he talking about? If you're asking that question, then you really, really, really don't have a good sense of gadgets, toys, and boys. In short, the Borg is a malevolent alien race portrayed on *Star Trek*. They assimilate entire species, turning them into part-organic, part-machine beings. The Borg are connected and act as a single intelligent life form—all the billions of Borg. When a Borg is severed from the collective through a disruption in its communication matrix, it's as good as dead. Its soul is gone. Now do you understand?

thing like that. He bought it, spent a lot of money on it, made sure it was carefully installed, checks every now and then to ensure that it runs well, and may even reread the instruction manual periodically. But look at or use? Rarely. Still, it doesn't matter. The generator's *existence* and *proximity* are what matters. Is this some sort of existential thing that Kafka would have gotten around to writing about had he lived longer? No. Not really. It is, as I mentioned and as I'm going to further emphasize and describe, part of who that man is whom you married and love.

If a man says, "I love you" just once in your entire relationship, that's probably not good enough. If a man buys you flowers on your second date and never again, that's not so great. If a man only does the dishes after dinner one time . . . oh, never mind about that. The point is that a man needs to demonstrate his enduring commitment and ability to protect the family in concrete and committed way. He can't do that by saying, "Hon. You don't have to worry about anything. Not about fires, floods, burglars, or somebody stealing our parking spot. I'm here to protect you," every day. That mantra being repeated daily, weekly, or even monthly would wear thin after a short while. And besides, no man wants to offer such emotional content so frequently: Gushes of emotion should be saved for occasions like solar eclipses and the reappearance of Halley's Comet. Mere words are neither enough nor necessarily forthcoming. But there's an even more significant reason why men would rather *demonstrate* their feelings through an action like electrifying the perimeter fence than by saying something with feeling. And that is: Words risk rejection. More than earthquakes, scorpions, or quickly fetching a newspaper left outside the hotel room and then having the door shut behind them and being stuck in the hallway naked—men fear rejection. Rejection comes in response to words, and it comes swiftly.

If you want to assign some jargon to this phenomena, let's call it *assigned behavior*. (I've always wanted to create a new word or expression in the English language and perhaps this will be it.) Assigned behavior is doing something that hints or suggests an unstated purpose. Assigned behaviors may or may not be understood or appreciated for what they are. And when that happens you hear a surprised response like, "But I bought the Hummer for *you*."

It's likely that this behavior—really, think of it as demonstration of affection—will result in a variety of odd purchases every now and then: a defibrillator, for example. They're now available in home models. The march of gadgets continues.

From a man's perspective *doing* something rather than *saying* something is a safe, concrete way of demonstrating his love and concern. He's hopeful that you'll see that, too.

All of this brings up a touchy subject: How do you discuss with your man the fact that although some of these purchases are as inexpensive as they are silly (that's just a perspective, not a fact), others are quite expensive and are going to make tuition or car payments that much more difficult. A defibrillator can cost well over $1,000 and how many 44-year-olds need one around the house? A Hummer—well, that may be even more difficult to critique. Generally speaking, the more expensive the protector gadget, the more important he thinks it is. You can't knock or disparage any particular purchase or a series of purchases (such as a new survival kit every month); doing so will directly and adversely affect how he thinks you think of him. Not good for the relationship. And you won't necessarily make any headway by talking about your overall household budget—though if done gently that might help.

I'm not suggesting that you give up or ignore what you think of as excessive spending, because that's not healthy for either your family budget or your relationship. The first thing to consider is: How bad a problem is this as far as your money, or lack of it, goes? Was that defibrillator a one-time purchase and not a trend? Admittedly, at over $1,000, it's expensive, but he didn't buy the Hummer—a very secure and protective vehicle. Nor did he create a "safe room," impervious to bad guys and bad chemicals, so it could have been much worse. If that's all that's happening, if the purchases are relatively minor, then maybe, just maybe—and it's going to be your call—you can live with it. But if not, then you need to talk to him. You need to tell him that you know he's keeping the family safe and secure (not that he's *trying* to keep the family safe and secure) but that blah blah blah. I'll let you figure out the blah blah blahs because what you say next is utterly individual.

There's one other thing you need to know about men and protective gadgets: These gadgets may genuinely make men feel more secure, safer, untroubled. As children, many men had security blankets, rabbit's feet, or favorite stuffed animals. From the age of one through nine or ten, they carried these comfort items around, not caring if the blanket became torn and gray, not fretting over the literal leak in the stuffed bear's sole. If you're a parent of an older or grown child, think back to when your kids were little. *You* noticed how ragged and rotten that blanket or stuffed animal looked and—admit it—there were many times when you were tempted to see how well it burned in the fireplace. But you didn't, and that's a good thing, because no matter how ugly that stuffed animal looked to you, your child saw something completely different, as if you were both looking at manifestations from alternate universes. You saw filth and junk; your child *felt* happiness through security.

I'm going to go out on a limb here—as you've no doubt noticed, that's not a problem for me in this book—and state that the longer a boy holds on to his security blanket, stuffed animal, or other object, the more he is inclined to seek out security gadgets as a grown adult. In addition, if his parents prematurely incinerated his favorite security object, he's even more likely to acquire security gadgets later in life. As far as I know, there's never been a study about this phenomenon, that boys who hold on to—or who have their security objects ripped away from their lives before they're ready—feel a greater need for security, but I feel deep down in my bones that it's true. Just talk to anyone who has had a favorite bear mysteriously disappear one day after returning home from kindergarten. "Oh, Beary must just have run away," mom said. She doesn't care, because to her the beautiful, stuffed bear is just a ragged rat. That one brief incident will have had a lasting, life-long effect.

How do I know this? I'm going to resist the urge to psycho-analyze myself (I'll save that for the talk shows, but you're welcome to speculate all you want in the meanwhile); however, I've spoken with numerous men who, in a moment of introspection and vulnerability, talk about how their security objects were taken away from them at an early age. They're sad about what happened to them, thirty, forty, fifty, or more years ago, and despite millions of other childhood memories, most of which have faded, it's this one—the one about the loss of their security object that is remembered most vividly. Many boys can quite clearly and perfectly recall the day their stuffed bear was no more. They can still feel the emotional toll. For many men, this was their first traumatic event; for others, it may have been the most traumatic event of their entire childhood. It's not only memorable, you can bet that many men have nightmares about this, or about events that are based on this, even decades later.

Men who had their favorite security object—a bear, a blanket, some other soft object—taken away from them before they were ready to part with it are more likely to need "security" gadgets as adults. They're in search of that lost stuffed bear, and this is a search that can never be fulfilled, in part because that actual bear can never be replaced, but also because the destruction of that security object (be it by fireplace or trash chute) was such a traumatic event. It's hard to describe the emotional trauma that little boys feel when the most important object in their lives ceases to exist. The adult equivalent would be having your family photo albums destroyed in a fire. There's nothing else as awful that's happened in a little boy's life, and nothing else he can imagine that could be as terrible. (At the age of five he probably can't imagine his parents dying or divorcing, so this is it: This is the big one.)

I have no doubt that there are more long-lasting, adverse side effects of ripping away a boy's favorite and sacred security blanket than the need later in life to pursue a quest for security and safety-related gadgets. If you look into your husband or boyfriend's eyes you can see a longing for something unreachable and a vulnerability that comes from knowing that it could happen again. Watch and listen and you'll begin to understand him more through the lens of this awful experience. You'll come closer to understanding his personality and what makes him tick; you'll come closer to understanding that enigma that sometimes seems to be protected by porcupine quills.

And what about guys who simply outgrew their blanket, bear, or rabbit's foot? Boys who may not have had their totemic object *taken* away from them, but who had their security blanket simply fade away? If you think you have escaped from being married to or living with a man who was traumatized by burn-the-bear day, you may not be as fortunate as you think. Men who never had their favorite blanket ripped away from them don't dwell on that sad incident, but they are still shaped, in part, by the loss. The longing that men have for security is hard wired. Men *need* a security blanket; they need comfort that comes from an object that doesn't disagree with them in every or any way. This need to hold, to believe, to have an object, is an integral part of being a man. Men may not worship a security gizmo, but it is very important to them, and men who have had a security blanket in their youth will feel incomplete without such an object.

Everyone feels incomplete, that there's something missing from his or her life, that there's an emptiness that needs to be filled. It's certainly true that gadgets won't take the place of a loving family; that gadgets don't provide the same physical and psychic rewards of a hike in the woods during a crisp autumn weekend; that gadgets can't even give the kind of emotional feedback that a pet dog, cat, or parrot can. But what does this matter? It doesn't really. People have a perfect right to feel better and happier through their toys. No shame should be felt at any age. The wide-eyed wonder that little boys react with when they see a train set under the Christmas tree is the kind of joy that they feel they can have and express throughout their lives, no matter what their age. This is a good thing. Some adults can reach back across decades and remember that day when the train set or erector set arrived. They can remember their first time riding a bike or playing miniature golf. I believe that men who can recall these wonderfully enjoyable events in their childhood are not only the kind of men who like gadgets as adults, but who are also made happier by these toys.

This isn't a substitute happiness—it's not taking the place of a family relationship or satisfaction at work. The happiness that comes from getting or playing with a new gadget is about as pure as any kind of happiness can be because it flows directly from the marvelous experiences of childhood. This really is the purest kind of happiness a man can experience because it's not conflicted or diluted in any way. Happiness that one may experience at work is far from perfect—work is never a perfectly happy place. Happiness that you experience in a relationship is also complicated with moments (sometimes prolonged moments) of unhappiness, confusion, and even occasional misery. Parenting—one of the great joys of life—bounces back and forth between elation and terror (with great periods of sleeplessness in between.) But toys—there's just nothing but ear-to-ear smiles. I'm sure that if medical research measured the endorphins produced by a ten-year-old when he unwraps that train set, the measurements would be off the scale.

How does all of this tie together? It's crucial to let men pursue their quest for security gadgets for several reasons. One, this pursuit of a new security object, which will likely manifest itself through the acquisition of multiple security objects, makes men happy. The causes of happiness aren't easy to quantify or explain, just as love can't be easily described through words but has to be experienced. But the connection is real and strong. You don't have to be able to understand or explain it to recognize that buying, holding, and knowing that you have certain security gizmos makes you feel happy. When one partner in a relationship is happy, that goes a long way toward making everyone in the relationship happy. (And the converse is even more true: When happiness eludes one of the two people in a relationship, the entire relationship suffers.)

There's an even more important reason that men want to, need to, and *need to be allowed to*, seek out and buy toys and gadgets that they see fulfilling a security need: Men need to replace the most important object of their childhood, their bear or their blanket, with another object that provides the same sense of security. They're going to search for that replacement object until they find it. You *want* that object to be a Leatherman tool, a backup generator, a Swiss Army knife, stockpiled medicines, purified water, or a remote controlled webcam.

Why do you want this? Because you don't want men to focus on you as their security object. You don't want your spouse or boyfriend to view you as an object, which is a very probable occurrence if he doesn't have anything else. It's going to feel odd. It's going to interject an unstable element into your relationship, because if he feels that you're not fulfilling that illusive and ambiguous security role, he's going to try and shape you into that role. You'll find that he's controlling, but you won't know why—and worse, no amount of discussion will change that part of your relationship. Because no woman can take the place of a Leatherman tool or stuffed panda bear (you know what I mean), he's going to try and try and try until it drives you crazy.

But there's an even graver potential consequence to his not having a security gadget that replaces his totemic childhood object: He might seek out *somebody else* as a replacement security object. And you know what that means. If you resist his controlling behavior, then he might look for somebody else who doesn't mind as much. "It's not you, it's him"—but that's not reassuring if he starts an affair, all for the want of a $50 Swiss Army knife. Yes, of course he should know better, and of course he shouldn't cheat on you, and of course you can't blame everything on a stupid, little stuffed animal from decades ago. All that may be valid and none of this absolves him of blame and being a jerk, but so what? The harm's been done.

For some men this connection between gadgets and being the protectors can sometimes fall beneath their conscious radar: They may purchase a fancy alarm system, a knife, a powerful flashlight, and other items that make them feel good, but they really don't perceive that they're actively pursuing the role of family protector.

Other men are into protector gadgets. They like knives, blinding flashlights, miniaturized Internet-capable cameras, and other devices that are designed to protect the castle. These guys openly congregate on geek forums and also openly acknowledge the relevance of gadgets to the way they behave and feel. And they actively talk about these gadgets and the role they play.

But no matter how consciously or unconsciously men pursue protector gadgets, these toys are an important part of their makeup.

Toys Help Relieve Stress in Men—They Really Do

I was on jury duty two weeks ago.

I was in coach for the second-longest trans-Pacific flight in the world just last week.

Taxes are due in nine days.

Somebody took my favorite parking space outside our house.

I was in line at the supermarket behind a coupon collector (a pro) just the other day.

I got a lot of spam this morning.

The newspaper didn't land on our porch during a recent rainy morning.

The phone rang while I was in the shower and it was a telemarketer at the other end.

Yesterday I was stuck in traffic for 20 minutes.

And I don't even work in an office. I used to, once upon a time, and I've talked with a lot of people who do, so I miss out on all the stress that accompanies working in an office, which I gather is a load of stress. But here's my point: men encounter a lot of stress during the day. Stress comes in all sorts of flavors, from minor annoyances to really big and seemingly insurmountable problems. I don't need to enumerate them, because you could fill several volumes with a list of all of the things that bother people.

Women get bothered, too. They feel stress just like men do. But they cope differently. Men frequently seek out gadgets to alleviate stress.

Why else would a guy turn on his car's talking GPS for a drive from work to home, along a route he can do virtually with his eyes closed? It's not just to listen to that female voice used by the GPS navigation system. (If he wants to hear a sexy female voice, half the DJs on the FM dial will do.) It's not because he likes taking instruction and following commands. (If he wanted to do that, he'd have his wife along on every drive. Oops!)

You beg to differ, I'm sure. You're thinking, "That's not true at all. The proof is that my husband would *never* use a GPS with a male voice. He will only listen to a female voice—proof that he thinks of his GPS as some kind of electronic flirting device." But that's a perspective born out of prejudice and worry and it's not correct.

And I can hear the next thing that's going through your brain: "If that's true, then how come he will *only* listen to a female-voice GPS? It still doesn't make sense to me. The only explanation is that he thinks he wants to sleep with the woman who's voice it is that's behind the GPS."

Now I think you're ready to handle the real reason: Listening to that GPS voice helps reduce his stress level. Part of the reason is that the converse, listening to a male voice, would increase his stress level. Why? Listening to a male voice would increase his stress level in many of the same ways that having a massage by a guy would be a mixed bag of stress and comfort There's a great *Seinfeld* episode (they're all great episodes, actually), in which George gets a massage from an attractive and very proficient masseur. He's conflicted and in the main feels quite stressed out from the whole event.

So what is it about listening to the GPS voice recite the same directions again and again, trip after trip that helps relieve a man's stress? What is it that makes him calmer and more content, drives up those alpha waves, and makes him a bit happier? There are a lot of little reasons* that when combined give life to the fact that having the GPS on actually works to reduce stress. Here are some of those reasons:

✓   It's a female voice. (Again, that has nothing to do with sex, but it does have to do with the fact that female voices are pleasing to men.)

✓   The GPS provides confirmation that he's doing something correctly. It's a pat on the back.

✓   He's welcome to disobey the GPS without any repercussions at all. That notion—that he can take a walk down the wild side at any moment, even if he doesn't—is reassuring and calming.

---

*I subscribe to the "lots of little things add up to a big thing" theory of living. What is that theory? You know it and you've practiced it, even if you're unaware that you're applying that theory. Let's say you're invited to somebody's country house for the weekend. Weeks ago that sounded like a great idea. But as the weekend draws nearer you realize that you haven't spent much time at home with your kids and you'd like to, there's a television special you want to watch, you're not enthusiastic about negotiating Friday afternoon traffic on I-95, and you're thinking of looking for a new set of golf clubs. There's no one reason why you'd like to change your mind about spending Friday through Sunday with your friends, but all those little reasons add up to one bigger reason.

✓ He knows what's going to be said next. Predictability has a lot to do with creating a stress-free environment.

✓ The GPS *might* say something different. There's always that chance. The possibility of something unpredictable happening has a lot do with creating a stress-free environment. (Wait! Aren't the last two reasons internally contradictory? Yes, they are. But so are men.)

✓ The GPS gives him something to do. At a red light (let's hope it's at a red light and not while he's moving at 65 miles per hour) or in the middle of a traffic jam, he might plot an alternate route, look for a restaurant, hospital, or amusement park (not because he wants to go to any of those places, but because he can). The GPS, by allowing him to fidget in his car, cuts down on the stress he may feel when he's unable to fidget at all.

✓ Having a GPS on creates an aura of security. The GPS is a backup system for the directions he knows by heart. Never mind that it's impossible for him to forget the route that he's traveled hundreds of times before, the assurance provided by the GPS can't be quantified.

✓ Finally, having that on-board GPS running removes any possibility that he'll have to stop and ask for directions. And you know how stressful *that* can be.

In many ways, a GPS that's up and running despite its absolute and utter superfluousness contains all the elements of how gadgets reduce stress in men. The talking, moving map GPS is the universal gadget. Let's look at this a little more closely.

It's not a male voice. I want to repeat this again (and this won't be the last time I say this)—the female voice that may or may not be embedded in various gadgets isn't as important as the fact that it's *not a male voice*. Stress reduction happens, in part, when things are introduced that directly reduce stress, but stress reduction also happens when you avoid those things that increase stress. The presence of a female voice means that a male voice won't appear, and removing that worry goes a long way toward cutting down on the amount of stress a guy feels.

Here's an analogy: Let's say you're flying coach from coast to coast. When you board, you're the first person to sit down in your row. So far, so good. Now your preference would be to have Brad Pitt, the Dalai Lama, or Dan Brown sit beside you, but chances are pretty slim *that's* going to happen. Instead some svelte accountant, lawyer, midlevel manager sits beside you (you can tell what kind of occupation the person has by the fact that he or she immediately pulls out work). That person's no Brat Pitt, but he or she is also not a 250-pound passenger who overflows into your seat. In other words, while you may not have the most exciting flight of your life, you're also not going to have a horrible flight. As every air traveler knows, whom you *don't* sit next to can be as important, when it comes to how pleasant or unpleasant your flight is, as whom you do sit next to.

In the same vein, that's why having a female voice lowers a guy's stress level: He's not going to hear a male voice. One worry (though that worry may be subconscious) gone.

The pat-on-the-back vote of confidence is another "little thing" that's part of the bigger package when it comes to reducing a man's stress level. Inside every man is a little boy who's just a tiny, tiny bit uncertain about whether he's doing the right thing, and who's especially worried about being found out making a mistake. Whenever men know that they're acting correctly, that they're not making mistakes, that everything is going as it should, their stress level drops a notch and stays dropped. A man who's not regularly reassured by a human or a machine (either will do) is somebody who's going to feel a lot more stress than he should.

Men don't like taking orders. On the flip side of that axiom, men like that they can disobey an order when they want to: Enter through the Exit Only door, park the SUV in the "Compact Cars Only" space, plug in a grounded electrical device into an ungrounded electrical outlet—being able to do these things (not necessarily actually doing them) helps men cut down on stress and anxiety. Again, not necessarily by a whole lot, but it's the cumulative effect of this and other stress relievers that can make a difference. As with knowing that there's not going to be a male voice present, knowing that it's possible to do what you want to do, to disobey an order, to be a free spirit—even if you're not going to act on that—is enough to help keep that old blood pressure down. Men hate to feel constrained, trapped, unable to exercise their will; and knowing that they can do something is often enough to make them feel calm and at ease. Knowing that you can do what you want do to (as in disobeying a GPS instruction) without anything bad happening to you (at least as far as the GPS or other gadgets are concerned) is comforting. And comforting is a stress reducer.

Certainty is important in a man's life. As it is with women, too. But certainty probably figures a lot more prominently into a man's psyche than a woman's. A woman, for instance, can be unsure about which pair of shoes to wear until the very last minute—and often beyond the very last minute, too, when she and her husband are running late for the theater . . . but I digress. Men like adventure and surprise, but that's a lot different from uncertainty. Adventure and surprise are things that men plan for—uncertainty is everything else that's unknown or can't be planned for.

Where do gadgets fit in when it comes to enhancing certainty in a man's life? Gadgets are predictable and often reliable. When you turn on your computer and click on the Firefox or Internet Explorer icon, 99.99 percent of the time you're going to connect to the Internet (Microsoft jokes aside). When you fire up that power mower, the grass isn't going to stand a chance. When you turn on the GPS in the car, you're going to find your destination no matter how distant or far: that's a certainty.

Compare that to what happens when a man, who happens to be a dad, merely *talks* in the kitchen during breakfast in front of his 12-year-old son or daughter. If he says something about the day's weather, that's going to be interpreted to mean that he thinks his daughter's not wearing warm enough clothes. If he offers to get a quart of orange juice from the refrigerator, the implication is that his son's not getting enough fluids. If he comments on something in the morning newspaper, then it's really curtains: He should be focusing on getting everyone ready for school. You could make the claim that it's certain that no matter what a father says to his 13-year-old in the morning, he's going to get a negative reaction—but that's not the kind of certainty anyone looks forward to, and it definitely is at least a 6 on the 1-to-10 stress scale.

Gadgets come into play here because they are a sure thing. In the morning, when all those bad vibes are going around, the toaster, the microwave, and the refrigerator light bulb are all going to work just as expected. Have you ever noticed that with some gadgets, namely computers and their associated hardware and software, men will sometimes grow defensive, as if you're implying it's *their* fault that a particular Microsoft program crashes regularly? Not all gadgets provide the same level of certainty and predictability, but those that do offer a special pleasure for men. Men are at least subconsciously aware that some gadgets either fail sometimes or frequently (computer software, especially Microsoft's) and that other gadgets fail to fulfill their advertised promises. But for the most part, most gadgets do what men want them to do. Press a button and a particular and predictable function is performed. It's not like trying to answer the question, "Do you like what they did to my hair?" which has no answer that's going to yield predictable results.

Worse, from a guy's perspective, than unpredictable results are results that can't be repaired. Results with enduring consequences. Results that no amount of intervention can ameliorate. As I mentioned, men are aware that some gadgets are more reliable than others—a new car is almost always going to start, but you can't say the same about a computer running Microsoft Windows. But even when a computer fails, it can be fixed. But even more: men enjoy solving a gadget problem, in part because things can only be made better.

Some men become dependent on their gadgets to relieve stress, and this can be a problem. For example, read how Sarah's boyfriend behaves when he's without his favorite gadgets:

> Hell on earth is an understatement. Once one of his five
> flashlights that he carries on himself (I'm exaggerating) fell
> out of his pocket and I picked it up to give to him once he
> noticed. Boy! Did he freak out when he noticed that it was
> missing. I guess he also didn't appreciate the fact that I
> pretended not to know where it was. I know all flashlight
> lovers would think that cruel but I just had to have some fun.
> However, I don't think I'd do it again—it was very hard on
> him. I seriously had no idea that he would freak out like that.
> He was like a child lost in a grocery store.

With gadgets men get positive psychological feedback either way: If the gadget works, then all is right with the world. If the gadget doesn't work and the guy can fix it, then that's even more of a mental boost. If the gadget doesn't work and the guy can't fix it, that's because of the gadget or technology's poor design or software. Besides, the process of trying to fix something, even when unsuccessful, is instructive. Men believe that they're probably learning something from the experience. (And they are.)

If you want to explore that aspect of a man's psyche—how he behaves when he can't fidget with a gadget—ask him to let you operate the television remote for a full hour without him touching the clicker. Just observe him during that hour, assuming that your experiment can last that long.

The Whole Midlife Crisis
Thing and Gadgets

What book on boys and their toys would be complete without a clichéd chapter on men's midlife crises? And indeed the clichés are abundant: men acquiring fancy cars, spending money on fancy watches, learning to fly, learning to scuba, and going on far-flung expeditions—these are just some of the trite, but real, activities that men take up to deal with their impending doom.

I'm writing this chapter for two main reasons. The first reason is the hope, however faint, that some movie producer might read it and be inspired to create a comic movie about a man's midlife crisis that's also clever and original—and based on my book. I realize that my chances of this happening are about the same as my chances of getting a Porsche or BMW convertible sports car. (Actually my chances of a movie based on this chapter are probably *greater* than my ever getting a sports car.) The second reason I'm writing this chapter is to dispel many of the false clichés about men's midlife crises.

Before I get into the so-called causes of a midlife crisis, let me talk about what a midlife crisis is supposed to cause. The first consequence is that the man has an affair with a younger woman, then is found out, and begs forgiveness. The second result of a midlife crisis is that one day, without warning, the man spends $50,000 on a red, convertible sports car. Sometimes the man who is experiencing the midlife crisis combines these two activities. But he's generally only forgiven for one thing, and he doesn't get to choose which one.

The whole notion of men having affairs because they're in the midst of a midlife crisis strikes me as a kind of rationale, an excuse. Men think that they ought to have a midlife crisis and that part of that crisis involves having sex with somebody who's not your wife because . . . well, because that's the rule. But it's just an excuse; there's no genetic imperative that forces a man to have an affair when he's 40 or 50 or whenever *he* thinks he's in need of having an affair. The men who do this are simply ethically impaired.

On to the acquisition of the sports car. Also *not* genetically motivated? Not quite. There is a genetic imperative to acquire gadgets, so the question is: Does this imperative increase as a man's testosterone level begins to decrease? Maybe. Although I was not able to find any studies that tracked men's declining testosterone and how that hormone's level changed after purchasing an expensive sports car, my guess is that it does—or possibly that it stimulates the production of another hormone that masks the drop in testosterone. I don't know precisely how long this boost in hormone level lasts, but it's not long. And this rise in hormone level is a weak one that can be rapidly deflated depending on that forgiveness thing I just mentioned.

There's pressure on guys to react to the midlife crisis conundrum. Men who don't do something about their midlife crisis think that others, especially those whom they're close to, see them as less than complete men. They're *supposed* to have a midlife crisis, and if they don't it's like being a virgin at age

40. People will look at them funny. There's also peer pressure: Other men in the office may have done something special to alleviate their midlife crises, and if you don't then it leaves you looking like a weirdo. The peer pressure can be considerable.

Many men succumb and buy expensive sports cars. (In all fairness, many also do it with the full knowledge of their spouses.) But not all men. Men who have been surrounded by gadgets all their lives tend not to need a big dessert—a sports car—if they've been snacking on gourmet truffles—other gadgets—their whole lives. The chocolate mousse cake is tempting, but there's no need to spend the rest of your cash on it. After all, you have some truffles squirreled away in a cool corner of your pantry.

To some extent, boys who have been surrounded by gadgets all their lives feel like they have all the gadgets they need. That may sound self-contradictory—after all, how could they have all the gadgets they need if they occasionally still acquire new technologies and seek out new gadgets? The answer is that they have all the toys they want until they see something that they especially like. And that thing is usually going to be a gadget that incorporates a newer or more advanced technology. The 2009 BMW convertible, which is newer than the 2008 BMW convertible, does not qualify as a new gadget; it's only an incremental improvement. (To many men, and to Madison Avenue, the new BMW is the coolest toy in the universe.)

When is a gadget not a gadget? When it's not desired. That's explains the apparently inexplicable scene that takes place every day in families across America.

HE: Is the owner of a zillion gadgets, subscribes to gadget and/or computer magazines, has placed various gadgets around the house because he thinks they're helpful (weather monitoring stations, for example), receives boxes from Amazon.com on a regular basis, steers all conversations toward computers and technologies.

SHE: Accepts all of this and offers to buy him the hot new gadget for his birthday.

HE: Says, "No thanks."

SHE: Is utterly dumfounded.

It's a sign that a man has approached midlife with a sense of balance when he can turn down the offer of a portable multimedia video player, a supersmart phone, a robotic butler, an all-ceramic Leatherman tool, a 100-percent wireless stereo system, or a BMW. After all these years, you offer to get him something that you think he would like, and in the same breath you're communicating with him on an emotional and subliminal level that's sure to further bond your relationship, and he says "No thanks." What's the meaning of that?

The meaning of that is near perfection. It's like the gift of the Magi without any of the gifts. Here's why: You're not only offering to buy him a gadget, you're actually communicating with him on an emotional level. Offering to buy a PDA may not seem like an emotional conversation, but trust me, it is. A man's relationship with his gadgets is inextricably linked to every part of his psyche. I hope I've gotten the point across in *Boys and Their Toys* that these aren't just gadgets: they are a divine component of who he is. You wouldn't know him without his toys: His toys let him fidget when he needs to; they give him not only an outlet for stress but a way to eradicate stress; they prevent boredom; they help hold the marriage together. But mostly they make him happy.

By conversing with him about toys, you show that you understand how important toys are to him, and that connection is revealing and real. It means you understand him, and it shows how much you care. He may simply respond by saying, "No thanks," but inside his brain all sorts of new neurological connections are being made, and these connections revolve around the good feelings that are part of his relationship with you. Just because these feelings and neurological connections happen to be a distance from the speech center of his brain, doesn't mean that he's not happy with your offer. He is happy. He's ecstatic. Feel free to do it again, because that reinforces the notion that you care.

A good gadget is something that the entire family can enjoy, something that can bind the family together. Of course some gadgets will, and must, remain the exclusive province of the man, such as that special car, perhaps the stereo, his PDA, that ultra-complex watch. But there are some gadgets that men purchase because they think that these will help connect the family.

You've no doubt immediately concluded that men who think toys can be fun for the entire family must be delusional. It would be like saying women buy shoes because they feel that's what most attracts men, and also the fancier the shoes the more comfortable they are.

Boys just want to have fun. As I mentioned, the midlife crisis is partly a fiction created by Hollywood and partly an excuse used by men to purchase expensive women and have an affair with a younger car. (Such is the perception of the midlife crisis: whether the man has an affair or buys a sports car is simply a matter of what he happens to see first.) But there simply comes a day when a guy feels that it's time to go someplace he's always wanted to go or buy something he's always wanted to have *because it's fun*. That's how my friend Larry Kahaner, author of a new book on AK-47s, decided to buy a motorcycle— and his purchase turned out to be just as he hoped it would be:

I know it's a cliché, but my new motorcycle is freedom and excitement for me. It's the opposite of daily humdrum. When you're on a motorcycle you can't think of anything else other than the ride. You are forced to be in the moment and pay attention to all stimuli. Unlike being in a car, you have excellent visibility coupled with vulnerability. Your senses are continually bombarded. You feel every crack in the road, smell every odor in the air. Rain and wet roads, for instance, are not just inconvenient; they're life-threatening challenges. I also take pride that in our digital age, motorcycles are analog. Taking a sharp curve is not ones and zeros, it's in betweens and shades. A little brake here, a little throttle there, and conditions change every nano-second. In my most honest moments, I admit that I take pleasure when people stop and watch the biker go by, pipes roaring. For a middle-aged guy like me, a loud motorcycle trumps the standard midlife-crisis sports car hands down.

Fun is okay. More than okay: Fun is essential.

As men approach midlife, they also become reflective. They realize that they spend a lot of time with their gadgets and that toys give them pleasure. There's a modicum of guilt associated with playing with toys, too: After all, time spent playing with gadgets is time *not* spent with one's family. Unless . . . unless you can integrate technology into family life and family play, just as the occasional Monopoly game may be a staple of family life. That's not a bad way to think about the way men perceive technology when it comes to family life: This is something to share. Men think of gadgets as being so much fun, and wouldn't it be great if they could share it with everyone! What could be better than that: Things that the whole family likes to do together.

Everyone's unique, and some men genuinely have a midlife crisis where they feel lost and where gadgets come to the rescue. According to Anita Baise, this is what happened to her husband:

> When I first married my husband, he tinkered with automobiles, put ships in bottles, and built elaborate model cars. (He was also a bit imperious with the remote control!) When the PC became standard household issue, he bought two, one for himself, and one for our daughters and me. He is a wise man. His first computer still sits pristinely in his den; ours has been replaced three times, a victim of too many female follies and foibles.
>
> Yes, sometimes he pays more attention to his toys than to me, but it has never bothered me much (except for one time when I slunk into his lair in a see-thru nightie and he failed to see through it!).
>
> By the time our kids were grown, the men on our block were losing their hair, gaining a paunch, and sporting flashy convertibles. Many were raising second families, having shed first wives like snakeskin in the ides of andropause. When he went through his midlife crisis, my husband bought a new boy-toy about once a week; I was relieved he was playing with his toys rather than toying with playmates.
>
> Men are just good at gadgets; they seem to have a special affinity for taking things apart, putting things together, fixing gizmos, attaching sprockets, etc. Maybe it's that males have stronger logical and kinesthetic intelligence, or maybe it's sort of a last bastion, an indomitable male province, a place where they can go where women will never be able to *outdo* them.

The problem, of course, is that despite the nice offer to buy him a gadget, chances are that the whole family doesn't want to go to Best Buy or Circuit City instead of having a picnic. Fortunately, it doesn't take much for most men to realize that they can do one thing or another: a *solo* visit to Best Buy or a *family* picnic (without the WiFi-connected laptop.)

There's a natural reluctance among everyone who's not in touch with his inner geek to shun gadgets as a way of connecting on an emotional level. For many people, gadgets are primarily a means of achieving a goal: receiving a phone call while you're not at home, finding directions via a GPS, keeping an organized address book, or computing taxes with the least amount of pain. Fair enough. But gadgets can also be a means toward the goal of a better family life, and that's what many men begin to think about as they become entrenched in midlife. If only they knew how to mix technology and gadgets. That's what the next section of this chapter is about: How to achieve better family connections through technology. (That sentence is destined to become some product's slogan.)

This is the how-to section of the book. It's a how-to for both men and women, and it is centered around the notion that done right, gadgets, toys, and technology can help enhance family life.

First, the no-nos for her. If you're antigadget in general, if you don't like a particular technology, it's okay to say so, but ridiculing the gadget is not okay. Men can have serious, substantive discussions over why a particular technology may not be better than, or even as good as, what's already in the house—checking the weather on the phone or on Accuweather .com may be quicker than having an advanced home weather station, for example, but not more comprehensive. If you (the spouse) explain why you prefer to spend 30 seconds listening to a recording in the morning on your bedroom phone rather than going downstairs and having to interpret the relationship between changing barometric pressure and wind direction, that's fine. But proclaiming "Who cares about falling pressure" is the wrong way to go about discussing your displeasure with this new technology. You can prefer your own, simple, only-makes-phone-calls cell phone without saying, "Why would any-one want a cell phone that crashes and has to be rebooted?"

Yes, it's true that smart phones such as Treos and Pocket PC phones do sometimes crash, just like real computers crash, but when you insult the technology it comes across like you're insulting the person who chose that technology. Do you want to do that? When the rental car's GPS doesn't have a particular destination in its database and you can find that restaurant in the $14.95 guide book you brought along, that's expected. When you accompany that revelation with an unwillingness to let him *try* and use the GPS even without that data, then it looks like you're jumping on the opportunity to prefer something on paper to something made of electrons.

And now what's forbidden for him: Don't buy everything you see reviewed on Engadget.com and Gizmodo.com and think that the technology will be welcomed in your home. Don't summon a family member away from doing his or her home-work or relaxing with a magazine to see the latest plug-in for your browser software or a fantastic website. Don't push a new gadget on family members unless you can explain in clear lan-guage why they might want to replace their digital cameras with a new version. "The camera you have is old and pretty fragile, and you may want to consider a waterproof digital camera for our trip to Belize's rain forest" is better than "You just can't take good pictures with less than five megapixels and spot focus technology."

From the perspective of a non-gadget lover, a new gadget is like getting homework. There's something new to learn, something that may be *hard* to learn, and a new way to make mistakes. Proposing that your spouse get a new gadget is like suggesting that the family car be replaced with a stick-shift car when you've always used an automatic. Sure, it might save gas and give you "better engine control," but it's more complicated than driving an automatic. A new gadget or technology *always* introduces a new level of complexity in family life, even if you think it makes life simpler or better.

Some years ago I promoted the idea of a home theater for our home. Home theaters are all the rage, and they are actually quite nice. Home theaters come in a variety of flavors, but basically they're large televisions with movie-theater-style sound systems, and which can play DVDs and VCRs and get digital cable or satellite reception. The problem is that the people who designed these systems designed them with one customer in mind: Rube Goldberg. To watch television requires at least three remotes working as a team: The television remote, the amplifier remote (only if you wanted to have any sound), and the cable remote to change the channels. You have to select the right input on the receiver and the matching input on the television. I won't even get into the complexity behind watching a DVD, but suffice it to say that I was summoned anytime anyone wanted to watch a movie.*

In all fairness to me, this wasn't my fault: I didn't design the system, and since this was our first and only home theater I had no idea that all the component parts would work together as nicely as Democrats and Republicans do in Congress. How could I have known? In my lifetime of experience, watching television has always been pretty easy. In fact, until I had a home theater system, the only difficult thing I'd ever encoun-

---

*If you're in a similar situation, get a Harmony Remote. Although I've refrained from pitching particular products in this book, the Harmony Remote, a television remote control, is a device that does as its name suggests: It brings harmony to your TV viewing. The Harmony Remote is the first, and to my knowledge, only remote that works everything and does what *you* want it to be able to do.

tered was programming a VCR. But my lack of hindsight didn't undo the fact that I had transformed a basic TV/VCR combination device into a majestic viewing experience with one problem: Nobody could watch it. Another car analogy: It was like replacing the family car with a helicopter. Sure a helicopter can go more places faster, but nobody can make it work. It's just an expensive gadget that doesn't ever get used, which is what our home theater was.

It's the job of every household's geek (which is how you're viewed periodically, regardless of whether you actually are a geek) to anticipate the possibility that each and every new piece of gadgetry will make your family miserable. That's what going from being able to watch *American Idol* to not being able to watch *American Idol* does.

Another no-no for men who like to buy toys: Watch the budget. Gadgets come in two sizes. Expensive and more expensive. It's not the one item that's necessarily expensive (though it may be); it's the cumulative total of all the gadgets you've bought. And evidence of your drain on the family's bank account can probably be seen throughout the house just by counting the number of things plugged into the wall. "Don't buy things with wanton abandon" means it's a really good idea to discuss purchases with your spouse. If you're going to have a fight over some technology, so much better to do it before you buy, when you still have some flexibility over exactly what (there may be substitutes) and exactly when (maybe some months after the tuition's due) to buy.

And the final no-no for men: When you acquire new toys, don't forget that you have a wife and kids. Enjoy your gadget in a time and place where it doesn't detract from listening to and playing with your family.

Which brings me to the nitty-gritty: What kind of gadgets

can actually help foster good family ties? I know that from what I've written it seems like the Amish way is the only way.

Outdoors gadgets. The stereotypical gadgety toy is one that's used indoors, in a dark place, and that's a very efficient de-tanner. Not all indoor gadgets are terrible ideas, but I want to start with technologies that are designed to work outside, because it's easier to acclimate your family to the idea that gadgets are good if they're used outdoors.

Right now, in 2006, the best toy that fits the bill isn't so much of a toy as a game: Geocaching (for more on Geocaching, visit www.geocaching.com). This is a treasure hunt that involves the high-tech, but now ubiquitous GPS, the quintessential electronic toy, as well as other technologies, including Google Maps.* The treasure is located in a box called a cache. Geocaching is lot more than a traditional treasure hunt though because it takes place around the planet and involves a wide range of clues including using longitude and latitude coordinates and offsets (providing coordinates to a particular known object, say a monument, and then having the treasure a certain number of paces in a particular direction).

Caches can be located under water or on hard-to-reach rock faces; they can be up in trees, hidden in caves, or anywhere. Caches have even been hidden in places like Rome's Coliseum. The cache-box contains clues to other caches, a log, perhaps little trinkets. When you find a cache you're supposed

---

*Google Maps are customizable maps that have their data available online. For example, you can take a Google Map (http://maps.google.com) and add data in the form of graphical pushpins for the location of every Starbucks in your neighborhood, or if that would be too many pushpins, you could add data for where crimes have been committed. In other words, you can take a map, provided by Google, and customize it so that the map displays what you want. It's brilliant!

to enter information in the log. If the cache also has a "treasure," you may take that as long as you leave another treasure of equal or greater value. The coordinates of caches (or offsets) are posted online, and that's where you start—at one of the Geocaching websites. Here's a short list:

www.geocaching.com

www.terracaching.com

www.navicache.com

So how does this work? Sign up with one of the Geocaching sites and start hunting! Get a good GPS, or better still, get several—one for each family member. You get to play, have fun, and commune with both nature and space-based technology at the same time. It's like taking a hike that's part of a puzzle and that leads to a particular objective. There's a mission involved.

Photo by Dominic Ebacher of Stephanie Furrer, who found a "microcache" in the Coliseum (photo released into the public domain, according to http://en.wikipedia.org/wiki/Image:Colcache.jpg).

Because Geocaching is worldwide, you can do it just about anywhere.

One of the reasons that Geocaching is so much fun is that you can't simply track down the cache by knowing its coordinates. Between you and the cache there may be rivers, mountains, quicksand, a lake—you just never know. If you haven't been outside in a while, this kind of activity is called a "hike."

Two groups are involved in Geocaching: the hunters and the cache owners. Cache owners are the ones who decide what to put in the cache, which is a waterproof box. The cache box can contain a Lego, a CD, a small stuffed animal, or even an inexpensive disposable camera so that the cache finders can take their picture for the cache owner. (Food is never left in the cache box because animals don't need GPS to locate food.) The cache owner is responsible for the box's upkeep. Sometimes boxes get stolen (though in the middle of the woods there's usually a dearth of thieves), and when that happens it's called being muggled by a geo-muggle. (One guess as to how that term originated.)

Many Geocachers also like to be responsible for maintaining a Geocache—as much fun as it is to go on an adventure in search of Geocaches, it's also fun to be surprised by who finds your own cache box. Each Geocache is registered on one of the Geocache websites, which is how hunters know where to look.

To start Geocaching, just get a GPS, find the Geocaching website you like best, gather up your family to look for or hide a cache . . . and GO!

That takes care of something you might do outdoors with technology. What about indoor activities? After all, if you live in the Northeast, it may be somewhat unpleasant to play outdoors in February, which is why you'll need a home theater system.

What?! Didn't he just write a long monologue about the

dangers of home theater systems and how scary they are? Yes, I can't deny that I just did that. But I want to revise my statement in light of new evidence. Home theater systems can be fun. As television marches into the digital age and as DVDs become ubiquitous, the television is being transformed into a "viewing experience." Whether movie theaters will continue to proliferate is an open question, but what I can say is that it's often a more comfortable experience to watch a movie at home than in the theater.

Once you've spent the initial $45,000 to set it up (only kidding—home theater price can be a little or a lot, depending how big a system you want), the cost of using it is the cost of an inexpensive movie rental, or even no cost if you watch free TV. There's no overpriced popcorn, no parking fee, and no babysitter to pay. You can talk if you want, or you evict a family member who's talking. You can pause, rewind, grab a soda, or do whatever you want. Home theaters are a family gathering place and can both physically and metaphorically bring a family together. Whereas a family outing to a movie theater is somewhat rare, in part because it's hard to coordinate everyone's schedules with the movie theater's schedule, it's much easier to coordinate a home movie presentation. And then seeing movies together is often followed by talking about movies together. Of course, everything I just said also applies to just watching a DVD on a regular TV (though it's more fun on a high-def wide screen).

And now enter computer games. When I first started researching *Boys and Their Toys*, I had assumed that computer games were part of the dark side of technology—solitary pursuits that tended to divide families. But that's not the case, and when you think about it, this makes perfect sense: If families can enjoy an evening of Monopoly, why not computer games? And indeed families are doing that with multiplayer games like

Guild Wars, Myst, the classic Adventure game, and World of Warcraft. The games that families play together can be enjoyed together at home or even on trips. These games let family members interact, spend time together, and then have something else to talk about afterward. If you've ever had an animated conversation after Monopoly, Life, Careers, Taboo, or some other game, then you have a sense of how much family interaction can be generated by intense play.

"The prediction that this was going to be an isolating technology turned out to be so thoroughly wrong," writes Professor James Paul Gee, a professor of psychology at the University of Wisconsin.* Computer games (and computers and the Internet in general) have a negative stigma that is very undeserved. Computer games can be uniting.

---

*Quoted in "Far-Flung Families Unite in Cyberspace—and Kill Monsters," by Mike Musgrove, *Washington Post*, April 20, 2006, p. A1.

Girls and Their Curls

*Women Like Stuff, Too, and
What This Means for Men*

I was talking about this book at a family dinner, when my sister-in-law remarked, "What about girls' stuff?" I was stunned. Sure, I've seen women with iPods, but the difference between men and women, at least when it comes to iPods and cell phones, is that women usually look at these devices as a means to an end: Listening to music. They're not into the iPod as the end itself. Women don't want a bigger or better iPod as soon as it's available. They're not going to be waiting, anticipating, expecting, and drooling over the prospect of a new iPod like men are. So what did my sister-in-law, Joanna, mean when she mentioned girls' stuff? It didn't make sense to me.

What she meant was: Shoes.

Of course. What else could it be?

Shoes. Women collect shoes. More than they need. Many more.

But shoes aren't gadgets. They're not wired up, they're not plugged in, they don't glow, you can't upgrade them, and you can't carry them in your pocket. They can't cut wood, and you can't travel fast in most women's shoes, like you can in a sports car. (They are expensive, like many gadgets, however.) Joanna pointed out to me that shoes are often the objective of women's desire: Not as a practical means to an end, like walking down the block, but as the goal itself. Something to acquire just because. Women want best, the newest, the latest and most exotic. Just like men do with their toys.

What are the implications of this? Does it mean that there's some common ground between men and women when it comes to gadgets? Can men and women use this shoe thing as a bridge, as a way to cement and secure their relationships? The clear answer to that question is: Maybe.

Let me say something important about this for the six men who are reading this book: Don't use the fact that your significant other collects shoes as a retort or a wedge. If you ever receive a derogatory comment on your laptop computer fetish or the fact that your power tools take over the entire basement—and you will—do not say, "Oh, yeah. And what about your stupid shoes?" Think about it for a second. Why does your wife or girlfriend have an abundance of shoes? (The number of shoes may seem like an excessive number to you, but probably not to her.) Don't focus on *what*. Think about *why*. And if you think about why, there can be only one answer: These shoes (or scarves, or sweaters, or whatever) give her pleasure in the same way that your technology or tools give you pleasure.

Life, Liberty, and the Pursuit of Happiness

This is more than just a political mantra: It's a philosophy that's powerful enough to cement a nation and a relationship. From the Declaration of Independence to modern life, these seven words have great meaning. They should be part not only of the Declaration of Independence, but also of every marriage vow. What we all need to recognize about our friends and lovers is that they are in pursuit of happiness. That's why you like powerful binoculars; its why she likes shoes. You don't have to understand the mechanism behind her love of shoes (and she probably couldn't explain it), but you do need to understand that it provides an important path to happiness. If it feels trivial or stupid or a waste of time and money to you, well, that's your problem. But it's a problem you need to get over ASAP. More than that: You need to appreciate her interest in shoes. It's meaningful to her that you really, genuinely, and affirmatively, like what she likes.

The shoes are her "toys." And just as you wish that your wife could share your love for PDAs and flashlights, it's her wish that you can do that for her toys. Doing so will go a long way toward cementing and enhancing your relationship. This may seem superficial, but I promise you, it's not. Most men who love gadgets of one kind or another pooh-pooh their wives' hobbies, dismissing them as something trivial or worse.

What does this mean in practical terms? It means that you should not only answer positively when asked, "Do you like my new shoes?" or "Do these shoes go with what I'm wearing?" but you should out of the blue say something complimentary about her shoes. It's not the shoes that need to be complimented, or even your wife's taste in shoes—after all, she wasn't the designer, just the shopper. What you're doing when you compliment her shoes is reaffirming the fact that you know that these shoes bring her happiness. You are adding to her happiness, and if you do it right you can create a nearly perfect moment.

What's a perfect moment? It's a fleeting instant in time where everything seems to be going right, where the only thing that's happening is the focus of that instant, where anyone and everyone around you is in the right place and doing the right thing. The perfect moment feels serene, lovely, important—and it's memorable. The perfect moment is something that can't be held on to because it's as fleeting as a hummingbird outside your bedroom window, but the memory of it can linger for a long time or a lifetime. You've done all that by smiling and helping her enjoy her shoes.

You may hope that the woman you love also accepts the way you enjoy your toys, as you're about to embrace her shoe affinity. But that may not happen. It probably won't happen. But even if she continues to ignore or snub your hobbies and interests, even if she fails to understand what it is that makes you tick, it's important that you do everything you can to show that you appreciate her toys. Even if the admiration or understanding is only one-sided, that's sufficient to make your relationship better. (There's always room for better.)

Tom and Ray Magliozzi, the *Car Talk* guys (www.cartalk .com), pointed out to this caller that "Guys need hobbies to stay out of trouble." That kind of trouble, they implied, includes having sex with women who aren't their wives. They told the story of their friend, Tommy, who had just spent $15,000 on restoring a car. They asked, "Does your wife have any idea of how much you spent on this car?" Tom and Ray continued their story: "Tommy walks over to the door that connects the garage to the kitchen, very slowly closes it, and turns to us and says, 'I have a post office box.'"

The woman who had called in to the *Car Talk* show said that her husband's old, beat-up car, which doesn't run, is basically "being used for Christmas decoration storage. I don't know how much longer to be patient. It would be nice to use that space in the garage or have a car that actually runs. . . ." Tom and Ray shot back: "You can't rush him. At some point he's going to say, 'Hon, I'm going to restore the Camaro.' And that's better than anything else he might want to do. He could say, 'Oh, by the way, I'm moving to San Diego with my secretary.' You *want* him to have that car. He needs that car. *You* need that car. Whenever he's ready, he'll do it. You're going to just have to tough it out."

And that's really the essence of the situation: You *should want* your husband to have toys. The bigger, the more complex, the more elaborate, extensive, numerous, the better.

And if your husband does not have toys, then you should worry.

Not all toys are created equally, and not all men interact with their toys in the same way. (There's a lot more about this throughout the book.) Conversely, there are a lot more toys than just cell phones, PDAs, fancy computers, and sports cars. That's something I've come to realize as I talk with men and women about boys and their toys: Toys include riding mowers, power tools, music collections, flashlights, old radios (even if they don't work), sports equipment, baseball cap collections, and, of course, nonworking cars. Basically, a boy's toy is something that he can use or play with. A narrow view of toys that includes only things that, well, look like toys, but this doesn't explain how men behave, nor does it pave the way to a better relationship between men and women.

A toy can seem like a total waste of space, time, and especially money to you, but it may at the same time be the third most important thing in a man's life—after you and your children, but before work. It's hard to comprehend that, especially if you happen to either hate his toys and hobbies or think that his toys and hobbies are preventing you from being able to afford to renovate your bedroom. When the framers wrote the Declaration of Independence they incorporated the phrase, "life, liberty, and the pursuit of happiness." They most definitely did not write, "life, liberty, and the pursuit of happiness, according to what somebody else thinks." What it is that he enjoys may be seemingly incomprehensible to you, a complete enigma, but in order for your marriage to last *you must understand and accept this fact*: Toys and hobbies are essential to a man's happiness and consequently to *your* happiness.

Men aren't like women. I'm not talking about either the obvious or the differences that comedians joke about. Women can't fathom a man's wishes and desires because men don't say what they are. That big, broken-down car in the garage doesn't appear to be anything special because your husband doesn't tell you why it either gives him happiness or will one day. Let me put it this way: Men don't ask, "Do these shoes go with my outfit?" Men have a clue that shoes make women happy (whether they integrate these clues into their lives is another matter), but women generally are clueless when it comes to what makes men happy (other than the obvious).

Men don't say, "Do you think I should opt for the Z4-hydro fuel injector or the Z8-norm plus fuel injector?" One of the reasons men don't ask their wives if they like their toys is that many toys are in a constant state of improvement, construction, or repair. It's not always going to be easy to divine what toys and hobbies your spouse enjoys, but fortunately you can pick up clues, if you want to see them.

Let's take the next step: Can women improve or save their marriages by this knowledge of boys and their toys? The answer is: Yes, if you're smart. Accept his toys, and don't disparage them. Smile at his toys, don't frown. It's pretty simple.

The Dark Side

Men Use Gadgets to Fend Off Meaningful
Conversations and Emotional Entanglements

Shoes again.

I mention shoes at the beginning of this chapter to make an important point about how men use their toys as a defensive shield against meaningful conversation and emotional entanglement. And that point is: *women do the same thing*, but for different reasons. They do, they do, they do!

It will come as no surprise to anyone that men and women are the same but also different. They're the same by virtue of the fact that both will die without oxygen, water, or food. They're different in all other regards (and even in some of the details about the essentials, especially when it comes to food). Why do women collect shoes? Why do women enjoy buying shoes? And why do women ask men, "Do these shoes go with what I'm wearing?" when they know that (1) Men generally don't have a clue as to what "goes" with what, and (2) By the time that question is asked, men are in a rush to get where they want to be.

Women say that shoes make them look pretty, that shoes

give them versatility when it comes to wardrobe selection, that shoes are the point at which the rest of their clothing selection starts, that shoes can give them poise, and that shoes make them happy.

Whoa! Shoes make them happy? A $200 pair of shoes makes a woman happy? What happened to talking with her husband, lingering over a glass of wine with a good friend, watching sons or daughters take their first steps? Don't those things make women happy, too? Yes, of course, but "that's different." We could spend a long time debating the differences between why women like to acquire shoes and why men like to acquire power tools (and many a couple have "discussed" these differences calmly over dinner), but what's important to note is that *shoes make women feel good.* They may not be able to articulate exactly why, and even if they are able to explain the way, men may not fully comprehend that explanation, but it does make them happy.

The side effect of shoes yielding happiness is that women don't have to seek contentment through their relationships with men, at least for the time being. (That interval can be as long as from the time the woman started shopping for the shoes until she put them on for the first time at home, or it can be a discontinuous interval—whenever she's looking at, holding, or putting on the shoes.) Let me say this again, slightly differently, because it's worth repeating: Shoes can be a emotional nexus for women.

And I'm sure that other things are too; it's just that men don't know about those things.

So it shouldn't surprise anyone that gadgets offer men an emotional refuge, and not just a trivial one. Men deliberately use their gadgets to thwart conversation and emotional entanglement. It's purposeful and willful, although it may also be such an ingrained behavior that it's also instinctive for many men much of the time. And that's the difference between what women do with their shoes and what men do with their gadgets: Although women may be using shoes as an emotional barrier, it's a temporary thing, an aberration fueled by something privative and instinctive. There's an inner conflict: The shoe thing versus their desire for feelings and conversation. The distancing that shoes cause is a side effect, much like the acid reflux that some people get when they mix whiskey with aspirin.

With men, it's a goal, and more than that, it's self-sustaining: Men like to emote with their gadgets. To the extent that toys are intertwined with who men are, their toys become permanent barriers to emotional entanglement with real human beings. And men will, sometimes, use these toys in a conscious way to thwart conversation, especially discussions about "feelings." They will use their toys as a preventive against "Hon, we need to talk."

This particular aspect of boys and their toys can happen with any gadget. It doesn't matter if it's a superadvanced notebook computer or a new power screwdriver—men can and will use that object to help them avoid what they want to avoid. And the more a particular device, toy, or gizmo enables them to do that, the more they are likely to play with it.

But not all men use toys in exactly the same way. Some men use their toys as an emotional shield chronically—it's a regular and persistent part of their behavior. Some men use toys in this fashion only intermittently, almost like women use their shoes. Still other men use their toys as a specific reaction to what's going on around them. It's this use—the conscious use of toys as a shield—that's potentially the gravest problem for a relationship and the one that I'm going to save for last.

When men use their toys only randomly and intermittently as shields, that should be looked at as a benign behavior. In other words, it's no big deal. In fact, if you (the wife, the girlfriend, the significant other) expect a guy to interact with you in a meaningful way, or any way, when he's polishing his car or seeing how far the beam from that souped-up laser pointer can go, *you're* the one who needs to, in the words of HAL from *2001, A Space Odyssey*, "take a stress pill." When the going gets tough, the guys go to their computers or garages or basements. There's almost always some "work" to be done on the computer's operating system, on the car, or on the water heater. Right? And there's no better time to work on those things than when everyone else in the family is arguing or snippy. Why discuss the core of whatever problems are going on in your family when instead you can fix a nagging problem with the water heater that's bound to make everyone happier? With a little luck that personal problem will go away, be forgotten, or get resolved in some magical fashion. But without hard work the water heater will *never* get fixed, and, in fact, will only get worse.

Men who use gadgets as occasional and temporary shields will eventually talk and deal with the human issues in their families. A man who uses his toys almost by accident to not have to deal with what's going on around him will return to your conversation as if no time has passed. In some ways, installing Microsoft Office—dealing exclusively with an inanimate object—recharges his emotional battery. Actually, that's a bad analogy: Rather than recharging his emotional battery, playing with a gadget drains his emotional tank, creating more room for more feelings and interactions.

Remember how you felt in school when you were studying for a math or history exam? It seemed like there was only so much space for all the facts that you needed to cram into your brain. The same thing applies to men when it comes to dealing with issues and having meaningful conversations: There's only so much room in the emotional center of their brains, and when that's filled up, they simply can't cram in any more feeling stuff or meaningful conversation. The tank is full and the fuel pump automatically shuts off. There's nothing that a guy can do about it; trying to add more space for feelings and conversation and family discussion is simply a physical impossibility.

Fortunately (depending on your perspective), men's emotional/conversation tank isn't hermetically sealed. It leaks. And this is where the analogy to a fuel tank departs slightly: The leaking isn't physical (obviously—it's psycho-physical, to coin a phrase). Playing with toys does two things to the part of a guy's brain that holds space for emotional content.

First, playing with toys causes emotional content in the emotional-tank part of the brain to drain—memories of meaningful conversations get deleted, opening up room for more meaningful and emotional content. I guess that this means you can think of playing with toys as a kind of computer virus that targets and destroys previous emotional content. If you're scratching your head, wondering if this is true, just consider (if you're a woman) whether you ever said something like this: "Don't you remember when we talked about spending more time together, alone?" And then having that question met with a response like, "No," or "I guess so." Well, what do you think happened to that conversation? He's not lying: He really doesn't remember the conversation because it's been destroyed or pushed out by that computer virus you know as "gadgets."

But as I said, that's not entirely a bad thing. Opening a space for new conversations gives you the opportunity to fill that space with what's currently important to you.

The second way in which playing with toys creates more space for conversation and emotional content is by expanding the space available for that. When people say that we only use 10 percent of our brains, what they mean is that we don't *want* to use that other 90 percent. This is especially true for men.

For whatever reasons, men would rather just flip channels on the television at supersonic speeds and pop back and forth between our two favorite websites for hours on end than discuss life and feelings with our spouses. Men frequently don't want to think (but you probably knew that), and they have learned not to. It's as if men's brains have collapsed so that only 10 percent is actually available to them. And they're comfortable with that.

Enter toys. Playing with toys opens new, vibrant neurological connections, like blowing up a balloon. Toys expand a man's brain capacity and fill it with fun, pleasure, and diversion. But what happens when the game's over, when he has to put that toy away? As with a real balloon that can't ever be hermetically sealed, the enlarged brain capacity begins to deflate, slowly but inextricably returning to its previous minimal size. Until he plays with his toys again.

It is like the eternal expanding and collapsing universe. In order to enable a meaningful conversation with men you have to catch the guy as his universe is collapsing. During the expansion phase, it's hopeless: He's playing on the Internet, fiddling with his BlackBerry, listening to tunes on his superstereo. After the universe has completely collapsed, say after he's been on the subway, where technology doesn't work, especially wireless gadgets, all that he wants is to touch and play with his gadgets until he's filled that balloon of a brain again. Only while his brain is shrinking do you have an opportunity to initiate and sustain a meaningful conversation.

This shrinkage can take place over the course of minutes or take as long as a day, depending on the nature of the man and the kind of toy he's been playing with. All you need to do is catch him during that window, and the next thing he knows is that he's unexpectedly talking about feelings, family, and the future. Remember, you need to strike up that meaningful conversation during the shrinkage of his brain, not when the brain's expanding because of gadget play.

And there is an important reason why the lines of communication need to stay open between men and women. Left unrestrained, men not only will acquire more and more expensive gadgets, but they will foist on their family technologies that make life worse. Here's what happened to one gadgeteer:

> My wife says she doesn't mind me being on the bleeding edge as long as she doesn't bleed with me. Which happened once when I tried to adopt VoIP [Internet telephony] for the household. Far too unreliable for such an important tool at the time. I'm glad she didn't take it too seriously. Similar things have happened with WiFi and cell phones, but she takes it in stride.

If the man is willing to undo the damage he has caused by his lust for technology, then things generally don't turn out so badly.

But the really dark side of men and gadgets appears when men consciously use toys to thwart important family discussions. It's when men sense that you want to bring up something sensitive, touchy, emotional, or significant, they whip out the BlackBerry or decide that there's a computer problem that needs fixing and that problem is going to take hours to repair. If a man uses his toys in this way—to prevent normal and important discussion—and does so consistently, then there is a problem, either with him or the relationship. If you see toys being used to stop all, or almost all, emotional conversations, then it's time to seek professional help, because this problem will continue and may eventually ruin your marriage. Fortunately, this is a rare occurrence, but one you should be on the lookout for—if not in your relationship, then with your friends.

For Some Men, Gadgets Are a Substitute for Watching Sports 24/7

*There Really Is No Such Thing as a Non-Gadget
Guy (and You Should Be So Lucky to Be Married
to This Kind of Man)*

This chapter is for all those women—and I've talked with a few while researching *Boys and Their Toys*—who proclaim, "My husband isn't into gadgets. He doesn't even own a cell phone!"

You're wrong. Being into gadgets doesn't mean that he has to own a cell phone, PDA, fancy laptop, expensive sports car, or anything like that. Gadgets come in all sorts of disguises, and if you've ever seen your husband with a power tool in his hand or on a riding mower, then he's into gadgets and you'd better read this book closely if you want to understand him.

Modern, electronic gadgets are what most people think of when it comes to boys and toys. But from a man's perspective, it's how the gadget makes him *feel*—not what it does and not what it is that's important. Let me explain. Let's look at a quintessential boy toy (and there are plenty to choose from): a multi-megapixel digital camera with more features than the space shuttle. Does this camera turn its owner into a better photographer? Not necessarily. Does this camera represent the latest and greatest? Yes, maybe, but that status is only temporary and the guy knows it. Is this camera a great camera? Yes, but it being a great camera isn't the most important thing.

The camera makes the man *feel* like he *could become* a greater photographer: It gives him potential and abilities that he didn't have before. He doesn't have to use the camera's features—that's basically irrelevant to its importance to him. But what is relevant is that the camera makes him feel happier. The same is true for devices that might not be considered typical boy toys: riding mowers, power tools, a stamp collection. All of these provide a kind of emotional support that you can't get from a living, breathing person. They make him feel good.

Which leads me to the other component of this chapter: guys who don't like to watch sports. These are men who can't name more than a handful of professional football teams, for whom the names Willie Mays and Mickey Mantle ring a bell, and who have figured out that Super Bowl Sunday is a great night to eat at a popular restaurant. These are men who don't know the channel numbers for ESPN and who are more than happy to lend a stranger the sports section of the newspaper completely unread. These are men who don't own any team logo paraphernalia and who rarely, if ever, drink Miller Light or Bud. These are men who probably keep the car's radio dialed down to the lower part of the FM band and who don't know how their college teams are doing now.

These are good men.

Only women who are dating, living with, or married to men who don't value spectator sports realize how great a thing this is. Men who aren't into spectator sports, who don't follow a team, or who don't have that sense of weird team patriotism have a lot of going for them. For one thing, spectator sports can be expensive. Tickets, logo wear, memorabilia, baseball caps—these can add up. Second, men who don't watch spectator sports may be a little more physically active than men who do, and they may be in better health because of that. They have more time to exercise. Third, and most important, men who associate names like "Oakland, "Miami," and "Dallas" with actual cities and not teams have a lot more free time on their hands to devote to their families. Spectator sports take a lot of time. It's time that can't be shifted. You can always move dinner back or forward an hour, but a game starts when a game starts. And I've been told that taping a sports game isn't good at all—it doesn't work. Spectator sports need to be enjoyed in real time.

But the fact is that there are men who hold no interest in baseball, football, NASCAR, soccer, hockey, basketball, or tennis. If these sports disappeared from the face of the earth, it would be no big deal at all.

So why is it that there are two types of men: The majority who like to watch football and baseball, and basketball, and men who don't? How have men who aren't interested in spectators sports survived evolution's cruelty? And how does this relate to gadgets?

Your humble author is one of those men whose interest in sports is less than zero, and who is proud of it. My experience is, from what I've been able to gather, pretty typical of most nonsports guys, and it went something like this: As a boy (a real boy, chronologically speaking) my lack of interest in sports led to a combination of ostracism and ridicule. From the point of view of many other boys, any boy who wasn't interested in sports was some kind of weirdo. And an opportunity to make fun of and exercise power over another boy in middle or high school was an opportunity that shouldn't be missed. Was this traumatic? Oh, yes. Was there anything a nonsports kid could do about it? Not a thing. Once so labeled, the label was for life.

So be it. The stigma and the personal problems that ensued from not being interested in spectator sports* are part of many men's history and lives, and they have learned to cope. But while coping, these men have missed out on an important aspect of life: "bonding" with other men through the shared experience of watching and talking about sports. "So how about those Raiders!?" is *supposed* to be followed by, "Man, Collins was really on yesterday, wasn't he?" It's *not* supposed to be followed by, "Huh? Who are the Raiders?" That response is itself met with perhaps a silent thought that goes something like this: "That's not a sports guy."

Most people think that other people are like them in certain important or fundamental ways. Religious people, though aware of atheists, can't imagine that the person they're talking to doesn't believe in God, for instance. Women who received what's loosely called a liberal education can't imagine that some women think that married women shouldn't work. American flight attendants think that everyone understands some English, so when there's just a blank stare in response to "Would you like some coffee," they repeat the question, only louder. And guys who watch sports just naturally assume that all guys are into sports. To the men who watch sports—and that's a majority of men—guys who don't watch sports are, well, weird. They're alien, suspect, and not normal. Watching sports and feeling passion about sports teams is just the way all men are. And so when they encounter a guy who's not into sports, these men behave differently around them. And this is what guys who

*Let me emphasize that I am writing about *spectator* sports. Many boys and men who have little interest in and much disdain for watching football and baseball are fit athletes.

don't watch spots have had to endure their entire lives: They're treated as if they're not normal.

Eventually, men who don't like watching sports discover this can be an asset, at least as far as some women are concerned, but that doesn't help with all aspects of their lives: Non-sports-watching men are still treated differently by their own kind.

Guys who watch sports can have an interest in gadgets, of course, but men who don't watch sports may have an even greater interest in toys. Toys, as I've mentioned several times, fulfill a psychological need—they create happiness.

But there's something else, too, about boys and toys that bears discussion: Through toys, men can find camaraderie with other men. They can bond through gadgets. And this is important: When men discover that toys, too, can be a binding glue, all of a sudden they have something they never had before—a way to connect and bond with other men. It can be with men who also shun sports, but who like toys, or it can be with men who enjoy both spectator sports and gadgets. That's not important. What is important is that through toys this sub-breed of men find that they can develop connections with other men that they never enjoyed before. This further reinforces their love of gadgets. Gadgets, toys, gizmos—they all become important in these men's lives in ways that were completely unimaginable before.

There are a few differences between being a spectator-sports fan and playing with toys, and subconsciously men who like toys but don't like watching sports will seek to bridge these differences. The most salient difference is that sports is a moving target—it's always changing. Sports isn't like Renaissance art or stamp collecting or even theology, where very little goes on. There's an entire section in most newspapers devoted to covering sports because there's so much new every day.

So how does this translate into gadgets? It might mean that your significant other buys a new laptop computer every few months, but fortunately, that's not the what generally happens. (One has to wonder, though, who does buy all those cell phones with those new features?)

Men need to keep current with at least one kind of "toy," be that a sound system, home theater, computer, boat, portable electronic device, advanced lawn-care technology, or golfers discussing the latest high-tech putter or titanium driver. Toy talk involves keeping up with advances and changes in toy technology. Listen to two men discuss computers (the most common toy that nonsports men get involved with) and you'll hear almost every conversation begin with something like, "Have you heard about the *new.* . . ." The new thing is the important thing; they need to feel that they're acquiring something novel. It doesn't have to be the latest and greatest all the time (though

Cell phone store. Photo by Bill Adler.

that's certainly not bad), but it does mean that he's acquiring stuff.

Guys talking sports. That's one of the few ways that men relate. Sports is the common language. But besides being a real phenomenon, this is also an overused cliché. Many men—and I mean many—would and do prefer to talk about gadgets and technology with the full force and vigor with which other men discuss the Steelers or the Red Sox. Conversations about gadgets can be just as animated, just as emotional, and take on religious overtones. (Just watch two men argue over which is preferred: The Windows or Apple operating systems. And throw Linux into the mix and you've got a small war to contain.) In our society, it's acceptable for men to discuss sports, but talking with any level of excitement about computers, cell phones, flashlights, or other high-tech gear immediately gets you classified as a "geek," "nerd," or "squid."* It's not just unfashionable, it's downright embarrassing to be known as a man who prefers to talk about bits and bytes rather than about passes and touchdowns.

I have to admit that even I, the consummate gadget guy, succumb to this failing. When our postal carrier asked me what I thought of last night's Nationals' game (apparently they're our local baseball team), I said, "It had its surprises. What did you think?" That seemed a way to comment on the game without revealing that I hadn't a clue as to the outcome of the game. I knew enough to be careful not to make any mistake that could indicate that I was rooting for the other side, because I did want my mail to continue. While it's unfathomable that two men, upon meeting for the first time, would say, "Are you looking

---

*A squid, a term popularized at Wesleyan University, is somebody who spends a lot of time in the basement level of a science library, just as a squid spends its time in the ocean's depths.

forward to GPS chips in cell phones?" you can walk up to any guy anywhere and start talking about baseball or football without any risk of embarrassment.

Life ain't fair.

There's no such thing as a gadget-free guy. Even men who have multiple satellite television hookups and season tickets to their home teams are often into gadgets in ways that they won't admit. That satellite television is one obvious example. A gadget that's a means to another end is just another gadget, no matter what. Some men prefer this kind of gadget, a gadget that in their minds does a specific thing, because some men feel that they don't want to be "encumbered by gadgets," and don't want to waste time "reading a manual," according to Chip Fisher, a middle-aged friend of mine who pursues outdoor kinds of leisure activities, such as hunting, horseback riding, and polo. "Gadgets, especially high-maintenance items, take a lot of time to learn to use." Men who have this view of life, that life's too short to read the manual, tend to like gadgets that enable them to watch sports; but they also like outdoor-related gadgets such as power tools, power mowers, and specialized sports equipment.

There are other gadgets that the self-styled sports fan pursues and even spends small fortunes on. Barbeque equipment is the center of that gadget universe. It's not just the $5,000 gas grills that sports-oriented men buy, it's all the accessories that can't be called anything other than pure gadgets. Take the talking remote thermometer that tells you when the meat's ready, or the weather-resistant grill light, or the motorized grill brush that makes cleaning the grill easy (if not a tad more expensive than using steel wool), or the chef's fork with the built-in digital thermometer, or the "handle-mount dual grill timer." Who would have thought that you can spend nearly as much on a grill as on the moon landing?

Grills and their accompanying accessories are not viewed as gadgets or toys. They're viewed as "essential." But that's the way that more traditionally gadgety men view their PDAs, laptops, cell phones, ionic room cleaners, and alarm systems. Something can equally be an essential and a toy.

There's another level that barbeque equipment goes to: Male bonding. Whereas men can enjoy talking about gadgets, comparing PDAs, or lamenting the slow progress of cell phone technology, other gadgets more actively promote male bonding. Brian Livingston, a computer book author and publisher of *The Windows Secrets* newsletter (www.WindowsSecrets.com) says, "I think that people have a strong need to bond with others, and that men need to bond in ways that are different from women." It's genetic—not just for men, but for women. Women also have to bond in ways that I've never been able to understand. For men, it's simple: They can bond over gadgets, over sports, or over what Brian calls "stupid contests"—things like belching competitions. It's these stupid contests, which are so pleasing to men, that may explain why it's so easy for them to bond over and get pleasure out of toys. Men are easily amused.

Sorry to say that if you think that having a guy who's into sports and not into gadgets will make your home gadget-free, you're in the wrong alternate universe.

The Meaning of BlackBerry

As I write this chapter, February 24, 2006, is rapidly approaching.

And by the time you read this, February 24, 2006, will have come and gone.

That date will either be etched into history as a seminal event in both technology and human behavior, or forgotten, just as 5¼-inch floppy discs have been forgotten. February 24, 2006, will be remembered as a day that everything changed—much like Pearl Harbor or when the aliens invaded in the movie *Independence Day*—or it will simply be recalled like a mediocre meal eaten on an Amtrak train. A big, incredible something, or a fizzle.

As I write this chapter, I don't know. By the time you read this chapter, history has been decided.

Oh, February 24, 2006, is the day that BlackBerry® service may be turned off in the United States. Journalists, philosophers, television pundits are talking about it: "Lawyer Bijan Amini is one of nearly four million U.S. addicts preparing to go cold turkey if a court later this month rules to cut off their fix—the system that runs the BlackBerry portable e-mail device," writes the *Herald Sun* of Sydney, Australia. That's what might have happened by the time you read this, because the company that manufactures the BlackBerry, Research In Motion (RIM), made a little mistake and used a technology that was already patented and owned by another company, NTP (and refused to settle with NTP—who knows what gadget inspired *that* decision), a judge has ruled that BlackBerry must stop using NTP's technology on February 24, 2006. Or else. Actually, there is no "or else": Research In Motion has to stop using the underlying technology that makes BlackBerry work.

Research In Motion says that they have a technological work-around and that when February 24, 2006, rolls around (and that's now history for you), their seamless fix will be in place and BlackBerries will be working fine. You know how that story has ended. I don't yet.

But the point I want to make is that if RIM has a good work-around, then this whole story becomes just another tiny news story in the history of technology. But if RIM's patch fails, then you may be reading this book, not under the glare of fluorescent lights, but through the flicker of candles: Such is the meaning of the BlackBerry. Nobody needs to be told that the BlackBerry's nickname is the "crackberry," because it's said to be addicting. People—and we're talking mostly about lawyers who work in Congress here—can't stop using them. I know at least two people, who shall remain nameless, who wear their BlackBerries on their belts *at home.* And you see it all the time: People, men, and indeed some women dressed mostly in suits, walking down the street, riding up an escalator from the subway, in elevators, at restaurants, pretty much everywhere, their eyes glued to their BlackBerries. And I don't want to know what's going on in the stalls in public bathrooms.

The BlackBerry reminds me of a *Star Trek* episode in which invaders try to take over the *Starship Enterprise* by addicting everyone to a sophisticated computer game. I personally doubt that's what the BlackBerry is being used for, but I wanted to mention this just in case, because we still have time to do something about that.

I personally don't own a BlackBerry and decided not to get one while researching *Boys and Their Toys*, but as a resident of the District of Columbia, the center of the universe for lawyers and politicians, I know a lot of people who own Black-Berries. Despite all this, there's something about BlackBerries I simply don't understand: Why?

Why is the BlackBerry so addictive? I mean, it's not chocolate or porn or a power tool. What makes the BlackBerry so special, especially when you consider that there are a multitude of other gizmos that accomplish the same thing, including Treos and Pocket PCs? (Full disclosure: I have a Treo 650 and a Pocket PC.) A Treo can do e-mail just like a BlackBerry. Same for a Pocket PC phone. There's really nothing that a BlackBerry does that can't be accomplished by a different device.

The BlackBerry isn't much of a status symbol, either. It's not like wearing a Rolex or having your car keys imprinted with a Porsche logo. It's not like Lacoste shirts used to be, or the newest Nike sneaker is today. Owning a BlackBerry, sporting one on your belt, is more like walking around with a flashlight attached to your belt: Utterly and totally utilitarian.

The BlackBerry doesn't even do some of the fancy things that Treos and Pocket PCs can do. Those devices can be used as MP3 players, movie players, and e-book readers. You can use them to surf the Internet in full color, or to play Sudoku, Scrabble, Monopoly, and hundreds of other games. But wait, there's more: With a Treo or Pocket PC you can watch live television and listen to Internet radio.

So why would somebody buy and use a BlackBerry instead of one of the multifaceted BlackBerry alternatives? I'll get to that in a second, but I want to give another example of how addictive the BlackBerry is. In the face of the near-imminent shutdown of BlackBerry service throughout the United States (February 24, 2006, is only ten days away in my timeline), companies (law firms, especially) are preparing contingency plans. Contingency plans? That's what companies need in the face of a terrorist attack with a nuclear weapon, a major earthquake, or the avian flu. But contingency plans because a particular electronic gadget may no longer perform to its full ability? Hello? What about the telephone?

And with that question rests the entire reason for the BlackBerry's success in addicting legions of attorneys, politicians, political staffers, and others: It works and it gives the illusion of freedom.

Let's explore that dynamic for a moment, starting with the notion that the BlackBerry works, and works well. The Black-Berry, for those of you who've never used one, is a smallish device (bigger than a typical cell phone, but smaller than a Treo or Pocket PC) that automatically collects your e-mail. That's the very short version of what the BlackBerry does, and the way in which 99 percent of the people who own one use it: e-mail on the go. (That can also include e-mail on the go at the dining room table at home.) The BlackBerry, in part because e-mail is sent to it automatically, is simplicity itself: In many companies and organizations the "IT person" gets the Black-Berry up and running, and from then on it purrs along happily, only needing a little top-off of electricity every few days.

So that's part one: Ease of use. Part two is the illusion of freedom. When somebody first gets—or is given—a Black-Berry, he or she may think, "Great. Because I can access my e-mail anywhere, I no longer need to be in the office as much as I used to be." (Translation: I can leave the office before 7 P.M.) And of course, there's some truth to that, just as there is some validity to the notion that having on-the-go e-mail lets you watch your kids' soccer games (actually be at them; watching isn't necessarily something that you get to do with constant e-mail). There's the idea that vacations may be more possible, because you can "be in touch if there's an emergency." With a BlackBerry you believe that you no longer have to choose between getting that brain tumor checked out and missing work. You now have the ability to check your e-mail while undergoing various scans and conversations with your physician—and that's a relief.

But it's the biggest illusion after the tooth fairy. The Black-Berry brings no freedom, no ability to spend more time playing, or vacationing, or being with family. Nothing like that at all.

And oddly, people who have BlackBerries realize that pretty quickly. They may find themselves taking a few extra days vacation with their family in sunny Acapulco, but they spend the day, head bent down, tapping and tapping the little BlackBerry keys in response to a torrent of incoming e-mail. You see, the BlackBerry not only lets you get all the same e-mail that arrives at your company's computer—it *makes* you get all that e-mail. E-mail's hard to ignore, and besides, isn't it just best to reply and be done with that e-mail, so you can get back to joining your kids in the pool, rather than just watching them (every now and then)?

And here's the answer to why: Men have been tricked, deceived, conned. The entire BlackBerry phenomenon is designed as a method of control. And it works. Just like a Pavlovian bell, when the BlackBerry summons, men comply. Can you imagine: Some hacker sends a message to every BlackBerry in the world, telling the owners to go out and buy a pint of Häagen Dazs vanilla ice cream. How easy it would be to manipulate the world's ice cream markets.

Some men recognize this control but realize that they are powerless to do anything about it. They're waiting for Dorothy to throw a bucket of water on the Wicked Witch of the West. When I asked my friend Howard about the BlackBerry's impending shut down, I expected that he'd talk about woe and misery, but his reaction was just the opposite: "It would be the best thing ever," Howard said. It was then that I realized that indeed BlackBerry users are waiting for Dorothy. Without Dorothy, they don't have a chance of freeing themselves from servitude; they have only the bleakest future. Not only will the BlackBerry survive (in some form or other), but it will evolve, too. It will become more powerful, more addicting, just as the Wicked Witch continued to acquire power.

Alas, Dorothy's not coming to the rescue.

Consider this: What if Dorothy had not thrown the bucket of water on the Wicked Witch? What if she *knew* that water would destroy the Witch and used this knowledge, this power, as leverage over the Wicked Witch of the East? Dorothy could have done one of those dead-man-switch tricks that the good guys use in the movies: She tells the Wicked Witch that if anything bad happens to her, somebody else—somebody whom the Witch does not know about—will toss a bucket of water on her. It could be anyone: The Lion, Toto, or even a flying monkey. Dorothy would have had even greater power over the witch and would have become more powerful herself as a result. There's more power, more control available in continuing the BlackBerry's existence than in turning it off.

If the BlackBerry has so much control over men, can women leverage that feature and use the BlackBerry or BlackBerry techniques to control men, too? Yes. And that's all I'm going to say about the subject. I'm not disloyal to my own kind, after all.

But the BlackBerry has some positive attributes, too. Not many. Well, maybe only one. But that one benefit is, I think, an important one in the scheme of things. The BlackBerry can help relieve stress, if used properly. How's that possible, you ask? How is it possible that the Devil's Toy can be a force for good in men's lives? Well, as I said, it's not easy, but here I go.

People in business get a lot of e-mail. I'm just the CEO of my own little life and I get an overwhelming amount of e-mail. Not just sometimes, but all the time. So much so—and I know I'm not alone in this—that I have a bit of dread when it comes to going on vacation, because after a typical vacation I can have over 1,000 e-mails waiting for me (not including spam.) That's scary. The mountain of e-mail that accumulates during a vacation (and I'm not talking here about Mt. Everest, but rather about one of those really incredibly big mountains that are under the Pacific ocean) is so great that it makes you want to do either one of two things: Not go on vacation ever, or never return.

Which is where the BlackBerry comes in. By being able to check your e-mail every now and then, you don't just reduce the amount of e-mail that you have to deal with when you get back, but you release some of the mental pressure that builds up during a vacation every time your thoughts drift to that e-mail. If you can summarily deal with just, say, ten messages a day, you not only make things easier for when you return, but you worry less about that accumulating pile of e-mail during your trip. (Easy to do without incurring undue family wrath when your BlackBerry gets a signal in your hotel room's bathroom. Admit it. You do it there.) And not worrying is what vacations are all about—that's not only good for you, but good for everyone around you.

So in a perverse, distorted way, the BlackBerry can make a vacation better. The only problem with using your BlackBerry this way is that it's hard to explain to your family how working during a vacation can get you to think about work less and enjoy the vacation more. It's the backward, almost contradictory nature of this that makes it hard for others to grasp. If I may offer an analogy that you can yourself offer to your doubting, scornful family members: Using a BlackBerry briefly is like taking a couple of Advil—you'd prefer not to have to, but it's better than suffering a headache.

Doing without when you've always done with: One of the funniest scenes on the planet is watching a man on vacation discovering that his BlackBerry doesn't have any reception or only occasional reception. In both cases, the guy at first, furtively, looks at his BlackBerry as the vacation proceeds from location to location, checking to see if there's reception. That's followed by more overt checking of the BlackBerry—not hiding his concern that the damn thing doesn't work in St. John's, Virgin Islands. At the same time, there will be a call or two to the office, letting the home team know that the BlackBerry's not working in the Caribbean. During those calls, he'll be told he's not needed and that he should enjoy his vacation. After a call or two, he will start to do that. I talked with one lawyer who was set free this way, and he reported to me that his son said, "Dad, I never knew you were so chatty."

Things are a little worse when BlackBerries only get occasional reception, as my friend Mark discovered in Hawaii. If you know that your beloved talisman's going to fail you 100 percent of the time, you have to give it up. But if it works sometimes, then that's going to make you keep looking and looking and taking advantage of those few seconds here and there to make it go. It will lead to what happened to the actor William Shatner in the *Twilight Zone* episode, "The Nick of Time." In that episode, aired in 1960, Shatner plays a young husband. He and his wife have stopped at restaurant in Ridgeview, Ohio, during a drive. At the booth in which they're seated is a fortune-telling device. Shatner gives it a try, and the advice is both uncannily vague and precise. So he asks another question, and another, and the questions that Shatner asks revolve around whether he will or should leave this town. The answers are foreboding, and Shatner sees the danger in leaving. Eventually, he overcomes his superstition and does leave Ridgeview. In the show's final scene, though, we see another couple being told by that fortune telling machine that they should not leave. Not everyone can overcome the pull of such an alluring device.

And that's what it's like for a vacationing guy who gets only occasional BlackBerry service: He's compelled to try and try again until he's satisfied with the result. Although men who are completely denied BlackBerry service usually overcome their inner addict, men who are treated to on-and-off BlackBerry service feel tortured inside—and so do others who are traveling with them. It's actually an amusing scene to visualize, though not necessarily to watch in person. How often does the guy look at his BlackBerry, and what are his facial expressions when he realizes that he's *not connected?* How often can he get away with stealing glances at his BlackBerry? And the really funny part: How high will he climb up a hill, on a chair, or up the side of a building to try and get good reception?

When I told my friend Larry Kahaner about this chapter on BlackBerries, he asked me if I knew about the "BlackBerry Prayer." As a Treo user (Treos are to BlackBerries as Apples are to Windows PCs), I'm a little unfamiliar with all of the attributes and mythologies concerning the BlackBerry and hadn't heard about this. But I can visualize it: Men seated around a conference table. They're holding their BlackBerries under the table (presumably so that nobody knows that they're using them, just like nobody can guess who took the cookie from the cookie jar at home). To type on the BlackBerry you need two thumbs, so the BlackBerry is held with two hands, which are also under the table. Everyone's heads are lowered so that the BlackBerries can be seen, and everyone's eyes are focused intently on the BlackBerry's small screen. It looks like these men in suits are engaged in serious, committed, spiritual prayer. And when you think about what kind of e-mails they might be dealing with, indeed they may have to pray.

What's both interesting and important to note about the BlackBerry, and some other gadgets, too, is that men become inseparable from these devices. There are possessive chains that don't let men separate from these devices. Also, men feel uncomfortable without them. There's an inexplicable kinship that develops between boys and their toys that can't be easily undone—nor should it be. In theory it might be better for men to be paying rapt attention at these meetings, but on the other hand, why? Most meetings are only 10 percent useful, if that, so why should the theory actually be borne out in fact? And it's not.

Perhaps the BlackBerry is a first step in our becoming cybernetic beings. Forget all those science fiction novels: This may be the way it begins.

The Wile E. Coyote Phenomenon

Why Are Men Undeterred by Gadget Failure?

I t happens. Gadgets fail. They just don't perform in the way that men hope they will. Men don't like it when this happens and they certainly don't like to talk about it.

Since this is what you're thinking, I'm going to mention this and get it out of the way: Yes, some men sometimes relate all failures to the possibility of not being able to perform sexually. And yes, there's probably a deep psychological relationship between men's fear of gadget failure and fear of sexual failure. But the link's not all that strong, because when it comes to gadget failure, it's the Wile E. Coyote Phenomenon that dominates how men behave.

To recap, in case you haven't seen the cartoon in decades: Roadrunner is the object of Coyote's obsession, presumably because the thin Coyote is hungry. But in the classic *Looney Tunes* cartoons, Coyote can never catch Roadrunner. Ever. Roadrunner's fast. To overcome the fact that Roadrunner is much faster than Coyote, Coyote gets a bunch of gadgets from Acme products, such as rocket-powered packs and super-spring shoes. These products don't just fail, but they fail in the most spectacular ways, often leaving Coyote dangling in mid-air, until, of course, Coyote realizes that he's actually in midair, and then that realization causes him to fall. The recurring theme is that despite evermore powerful technology, Coyote is unable to capture Roadrunner and remains hungry.

Behind the Wile E. Coyote Phenomenon is the notion that if the first gadget doesn't work, another one will. And there's an endless supply of gadgets available to continue the mission. One has to wonder what's more important to Coyote: resolving the Roadrunner issue or taking advantage of it to try out these new gadgets? Coyote doesn't seem to relish the hunt; and he's certainly hungry, which logically means he should pursue other prey. But he doesn't. Coyote could stop but chooses not to. Wile E. Coyote's quest is forever. Why?

The answer rests with Coyote's nature. He is compelled by a complex need that's in part fueled by a desire to acquire better gadgets. Rather than Roadrunner being the object and Acme Products being the means, in reality it's the other way around: Acme Products is the goal, and Roadrunner is the excuse, the rationale.

Despite the inevitability of failure, Coyote is going to acquire a new gadget. Hopefully, the next one will work. Is Coyote an optimist? Maybe. Maybe not. But optimism isn't the force that drives him. What compels Coyote to get gadget after gadget is the pleasure he derives from trying out new gadgets.

With men, it's a similar thing: the toys are the goal, and their various functions are the way men rationalize acquiring these toys. Accomplishing the mission is often not the objective. After all, a sports car and a minivan will get you to the office in roughly the same time. A superfast computer and a superslow one will both work fine when it comes to Googling.

Wile E. Coyote likes what he's doing. He likes his life, and he likes his toys, even though they don't away work. All men have Wile E. Coyote in them, because they simply like toys.

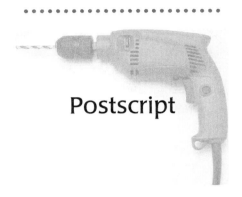

Postscript

It's not ironic that my latest and theoretically greatest gadget arrived by FedEx just a week before this manuscript was due. (Thus delaying it even more. Oh, well.) That a new gadget would arrive at my home on any random day is not at all surprising to me or my family. The doorbell rings, it's a delivery, I rush downstairs, grab the box, return to my office, and that's the last anyone sees of me for the next five hours.

The gadget that had the nerve to interfere with my work was an HTC Wizard, a high-powered smart phone with Bluetooth, WiFi, a keyboard that slides out the side, stereo output, 1.3 megapixel camera, and more. See why I was so excited about this package?

But what is ironic is that after a few days I wanted to throw it in the lake. I *hated* the thing. *That's* ironic—as I'm nearing the end of a book about gadgets, a gadget would arrive that I couldn't stand to be in the same room with.

Don't get me wrong. I *wanted* to like the HTC Wizard. I thought I *would like* the HTC Wizard. There was nothing in the world that stood between me and liking, if not loving, this incredible cell phone. Except for the simple truth that I just didn't like it.

And I'll tell you why. It had nothing to do with a lack of bells and whistles. The HTC Wizard, with its built-in WiFi connectivity, can surf the Internet at over ten times the speed of my Treo 650, last year's state-of-the-art cell phone. It has a better display. It had voice dialing: "Call home" and home is called. It has better multimedia playback.

The problem was that the HTC Wizard just isn't as easy to use as the Treo 650. With the Treo 650 you can do everything with one hand: from making phone calls to checking your e-mail to listening to tunes like you do on an iPod. With the HTC Wizard, you almost always need a stylus or two hands or both to do anything. And that brilliant sliding keyboard? Well, it's cool and it works really well, and it's as close as you can get to having a full keyboard on a cell phone, but having to rotate my phone 90 degrees (after sliding out the keyboard) every time I want to type an e-mail, text message, or note, is just too unnatural.

The HTC Wizard is a great gadget for other guys, I'm sure. It's just not right for me.

Dare I say it? Sometimes a gadget that works well is better than a newer, shinier, but unproven gadget.

I realize that if you're not a gadget person, both the Treo 650 and HTC Wizard are pretty much identical (and possibly irrelevant) from your perspective, which may be that they're both cell phones that went overboard on steroids. But trust me when I say that the Treo 650 is last year's latest and greatest and the HTC Wizard is what's number one now.

The hardest thing when it comes to gadgets isn't passing up a new gadget because its too expensive, too big, too flashy, or takes too much time to learn. The hardest thing for me is knowing that I've gone a step *backward* in technology. I actually got rid of the more advanced device and returned to the older gizmo. Is it like forsaking a Touch-Tone phone for a telephone with a rotary dial? Perhaps. Maybe I'm getting weak at the knees when it comes to wanting and needing new toys. I hope not. Because if I lose my desire for new, great gadgets, what will I have left? Just family and friends?

Index